Family Business by the Numbers: How Financial Statements Impact Your Business

Norbert E. Schwarz

FAMILY ENTERPRISE PUBLISHERS

Division of The Family Business Consulting Group, Inc.

©2004

ISBN 1-891652-14-1

Family Business by the Numbers:
How Financial Statements Impact Your Business
Norbert E. Schwarz

Copyright 2004 by Family Enterprise Publishers®
    1220-B Kennestone Circle
    Marietta, GA 30066
    800-551-0633
    www.efamilybusiness.com
Jacket design by Claudia Griffiths, Griff Graphics.

TABLE OF CONTENTS

INTRODUCTION

. . . . 1

CHAPTER 1

What Are Annual Reports All About?. 3

CHAPTER 2

Overview of the Annual Financial Statement 9

CHAPTER 3

The Balance Sheet: Overview 13

CHAPTER 4

The Balance Sheet: Assets. 19

CHAPTER 5

The Balance Sheet: Liabilities and Owners' Equity 25

CHAPTER 6

The Balance Sheet: Five-Year Comparisons 31

CHAPTER 7

The Income Statement 37

CHAPTER 8

The Statement: Five-Year Comparisons 49

CHAPTER 9

The Cash Flow Statement 59

CHAPTER 10

Financial Ratios and Analysis Tools 71

CHAPTER 11

Aftermath 91

CHAPTER 12

The Next Steps 93

ACCOUNTING TERMS

. . . . 99

INDEX

. . . . 105

INTRODUCTION

Something was wrong—a crime had been committed or was about to happen. Sherlock Holmes set about collecting seemingly unimportant pieces of information: the spacing of footsteps, an item of clothing, a small clod of dirt. Then his logical mind began piecing together these apparently disconnected facts into a vivid picture of criminal activities.

In like manner, when two young heirs to their family business wanted to investigate whether their company is in trouble, financial expert Bob Holmes starts by collecting facts from the Balance Sheets, Income Statements, Cash Flows Statements and Ratio Analyses. Sue and Greg (the young heirs) initially roll their eyes at these seemingly dull and obscure pieces of information. However, they soon become caught up in the "chase" as Holmes begins helping them to piece these bits of information into a sharpening picture of their company's strengths and potential weakness.

As you follow this story, you will go beyond merely learning the financial terms to learning how to use financial statements as an investigative tool for uncovering the dynamics of a business.

Norb Schwarz

CHAPTER 1

What Are Annual Reports All About?

Suspicions

The pair certainly did not look like the owners of a hundred-million-dollar corporation. The woman could not be more than five years out of college, and her long, straight hair, multicolored clothes, and flamboyant jewelry suggested an artist. The man looked like a graduate student who, judging from his denim shirt and jacket, had just changed from blue jeans into a pair of wash pants.

The banker offered his hand. "We meet at last. I'm Bob Holmes."

"I'm Sue Monahan, and this is my cousin, Greg Ferris. We've come to talk to you about our family's business, FerMon Lamp Company."

Holmes ushered them to a round conference table and sat they sat down. "Frankly, I expected to see you four years ago, after your parents died in that unfortunate accident. I was designated as your mentor, to help you prepare for the day your trusts end—which, as I remember, is when you celebrate your thirtieth birthdays. However, I may not be as helpful now, since I've been off the company's board of directors for three years. You may want to have someone still with the company mentor you on this."

"Frankly, Mr. Holmes, we wanted to consult with someone not currently with the company, and our parents' trust in you makes you the logical choice," Sue explained.

"Actually," Greg interrupted, "we've come to put Sue's mind to rest about the business. She seems to have picked up the notion that it's in some kind of trouble."

"Why do you think something is wrong?"

"Well, I don't know much about business, so I'm not sure. However, I have heard some disturbing remarks from people who work there, and I've noticed a few things that don't look right, like a lot of dusty cartons crowded into the finished-goods area.

"I'm a product designer and, until recently, I had seldom visited the plants. A couple of months ago, I thought I'd try my hand at designing a few lamps and was given a part-time position at the low-cost subsidiary as a trial. At the main plant, I was told that they pretty much stick to their 'classic' lines and, in any case, were all tied up in reconfiguring them. I eventually discovered that this meant finding ways of making the lamps more cheaply. Don't you think that could undermine a company built on its reputation for high quality, Mr. Holmes?"

"Well, that would depend upon how and why it was being done. Improved manufacturing techniques or the elimination of costly but unessential materials could make the lamps more competitive. On the other hand, making lamps that look cheap and don't work well would undermine the company's reputation for quality. It's hard to tell much from isolated facts."

"Exactly," Greg chimed in. "Look, Sue, we all know about old-line companies whose prices rose so high that nobody would buy their outdated products. If the executives want to make a few changes, I'm sure they know what they're doing. Our company's going steady as a clock—always pays our dividends on time."

"But they have gone down a lot the last couple of years."

"Well, we can't always expect outstanding years, and sometimes a company has to devote its profits to future growth. We're still getting plenty to live on."

"And that's what's important to Greg. It's paying his way through medical school and will let him set up his practice."

"And let you dabble at your artsy projects."

Holmes moved quickly to refocus the discussion. "Are there any other observations that disturbed you?"

"Well, a couple of people who have worked at the company for many years told me several things that started me worrying. For example, one of them said that most of the profits are coming from the subsidiary making cheaper lamps, but that there are rumors about this division's being sold. When I met the president and asked about this, he seemed a little evasive and asked where I'd heard that, which made me worry about compromising the people who'd confided in me. He said no such decision has been made but that one always has to consider every option for improving the overall business. I fail to see the wisdom in selling off the only part of the business that's making money.

"Another thing my source told me is that the company has begun borrowing significant amounts of money during the past two or three years. Our parents always took pride in being debt-free."

Numbers: Objective and Standardized Information

Holmes reflected on this for a moment. "These could be significant factors. It's hard to tell without further information. For example, borrowing money and selling assets to improve the company's other capabilities is an excellent, established way of keeping a company competitive and expanding it. On the other hand, raising money these ways simply to meet ordinary expenses and to pay dividends would eventually leave you with no equity—it would milk the business dry." He turned to Sue. "Thanks for sending me the annual reports I requested on the telephone. I have been able to compile them into five-year statements that we can examine after going over the financial statements for last year."

The cousins sighed, and Sue exclaimed, "Really, Mr. Holmes, I don't see how a bunch of abstract figures can tell you much about what people are doing in a complex company."

"Especially," Greg added, "when the numbers are all related to weird things like 'debentures' and 'accrued earnings.'"

Holmes chuckled. "Yes, financial experts have their special terminology, as do most professionals, including artists and doctors. And speaking of doctors, Greg, don't numbers play a central role in evaluating a patient's health? There are body temperature, blood pressure, all kinds of numbers from blood tests, and the graphs from electrocardiograms. Why do doctors reduce the complex operations of our bodies to numbers?"

Greg smiled. "I remember one professor who talked about how early doctors used to evaluate patients by estimating how pale or flushed they looked and how warm or cool they felt. The 'tests' consisted of evaluating the colors and degrees of warmth. It was pretty subjective."

Holmes nodded. "It's the same with evaluating the health of a business. Of course, numbers don't tell us everything. Just as the doctor has to observe, touch and talk with the patient, so one has to observe what is going on in a business and talk to people there, as Sue has done. Nevertheless, the numbers that have been standardized for annual reports are a fast way of getting a pretty good overall picture of how a company is doing. It also enables us to compare its performance to that of other companies."

Comparing Numbers

"Don't tell me we have to study reports from other companies, too!" Sue objected.

"Not usually, though you might want to if you were tracking down a specific problem, like excessive expenses or poor sales. Suppose profits suddenly fell one year. It would be helpful to know whether this happened in the economy as a whole or in your particular industry. Or suppose that one of your competitors suddenly started taking away a lot of business from you: you might want to not only examine its products but see from their report whether it has lowered its costs, increased its investments, and so on."

"You seem to be saying that these reports provide a shortcut to evaluating a company, but they don't seem very short," Sue commented.

"Yeah, why can't they just say how much the company is worth and how much money it's making?" Greg added.

"Of course, we do, but a simple statement would not tell you enough. For example, suppose a business had three million dollars in cash at the end of the year. Would you say it was doing well?"

"Sure," they said.

"But suppose that in one month it had to pay off five million dollars for loans and purchases?"

"Maybe not so well," Sue murmured.

"Suppose further that, in three months, some long-term investments would mature and pay four million dollars? Suppose we had to replace expensive equipment or a plant within a year? I could go on, but you can see that we need quite a few items of information before we can form an adequate picture of a business—or even fully understand the meaning of an individual number."

"A number is a number, isn't it?" Greg objected. "I mean, isn't that why we use numbers, because they are exact?"

"Yes, but their meaning can vary drastically. Is a very high blood-pressure reading always bad?"

"When you take it in a regular examination, yes. I suppose you mean that a high measurement would be expected, even good, right after a stress test."

"Exactly. Now, take 'Accounts Receivable'—money that customers owe for goods shipped to them. If this amount increases by twenty percent in the latest annual report, what does it mean?"

"I suppose it could mean that sales have gone up, which would be good," Sue offered. "Or it could mean that customers aren't paying their bills, which would be bad."

"You've got it. One way of testing this is to see whether Net Sales have gone up in the same way. By comparing various figures in the report, we can find out a surprising number of things about how well a company is doing."

The cousins groaned. "Do you mean to say that we not only have to go through all those figures but also have to make further calculations with them?" Greg demanded.

"I'm afraid so. I might as well give you the rest of the bad news: sometimes you will have to look up some more detailed information to clear up the questions you raise when going through the reports."

A Sense of Direction

"When I started riding lessons, my instructor said that I had to direct the horse with a few simple actions, like tugging the reins and exerting pressure with my legs and feet. The horse would then do all the work. However, if I didn't show the animal who is boss, then the horse might take me where I don't want to go.

"Similarly, you have executives and workers who will handle almost all of the work for you, but, as owners, you will have to spend time going over reports, attending meetings and visiting the plants to make sure the company is achieving its goals. I assure you, this is a lot easier than starting a new business, like your grandparents did, or building it up, as your parents did."

"I suppose," Sue said, "but that sounds so coldly calculating, almost exploitive—how much we can get out of others."

"It doesn't have to be. Making sure a company is running soundly also protects the livelihoods of all those who work for it, and provides the means for any improvements you'd like to make for them."

Levels of Information

"Okay," Greg agreed, "but exactly how deeply do we have to dig into these reports, and how much research do we have to do? I hope we won't have to worry about how many paper clips the office is using."

"Not unless you hear of something like the Department of Defense's paying $700 for an ordinary hammer," Holmes laughed. "Ordinarily, the bookkeepers take care of recording and totaling data like this. Trying to evaluate countless small items would prove exhausting and would leave one more confused than enlightened about what was going on in the overall business."

"Yeah," Greg agreed. "I mean, what would you conclude from finding out that we spent less on paper clips in March but more on pencils in August?"

"Exactly. Now, when we categorize these expenses, say, come up with totals like 'Office Supplies,' 'Office-Building Expenses,' and 'Office Salaries,' we have some information that begins to show the larger events in the company. We start with Data which includes the bookkeeping entries that are the foundation for developing the numbers on the financial statements. When the data are accumulated to meaningful statements and reports, we have Information. When we are able to understand the financial statements, we have Knowledge. When we are able to make intelligent decisions using the information we have, we achieve the last element in the financial decision making process, Wisdom."

"True," Sue said, "but that's still a lot of detail to go through."

"That's why, in the annual report, we further consolidate this information into more inclusive categories, like 'Administrative Expenses,' or something ever broader, like 'Selling, General, and Administrative Expenses.' This and other broad categories like 'Net Sales' and 'Operating Expenses' give us a more manageable picture of the business."

Sue frowned in thought. "I can see how that kind of statement could work—whether sales are increasing enough to cover increasing expenses or whether one area of expenses is getting out of control."

"You have now arrived at knowledge, where you start working with information and arrive at a real understanding of what is happening in the company."

"And that kind of understanding tells you when you need more detailed information," Greg added. "If Administrative Expenses are getting too big compared with, say, Net Sales and Manufacturing Expenses, then one begins digging to find out why."

"Exactly. Hopefully, one will not have to go down to the level of paper clips, but one might discover that an older building is costing too much to maintain, or that people need better computers and software to work more efficiently, or that the officers are rewarding themselves too generously. Arriving at these insights and learning to deal with them is the highest, but hardest-to-reach, plateau of wisdom."

A Company's Annual "Physical"

Greg was running with an idea. "You might say that the annual report is kind of like a physical exam: it covers the major systems and, when the results look abnormal, one orders further, more detailed, tests."

"I like that," Holmes said. "I'll have to use that definition with some of my clients."

He paged through the reports Sue had given him. "Now that we have gone through the general ideas of what annual reports cover and how they are related to other information about a company, it is time to look at them in more detail. We'll start by looking at the big picture and see whether that shows anything corresponding to your suspicions, Sue."

CHAPTER 2

Overview of the Annual Financial Statement

Reliability

"I gather," Greg said, "that the Balance Sheet tells how much the company is worth, and that the Income Statement tells how much money it is making. So which one do we begin with?"

Holmes nodded. "You're right about the general meaning of those two parts. There are also three other significant items—Cash Flow, Financial Analysis, and the notes to the financial statements, which, like other fine print, often contain very important information. For example, a note might explain an atypical source of profit or loss."

"Why should anything be easy?" Sue groaned.

Holmes smiled. "Oh, it's not that bad, especially for a medium-sized company like FerMon. However, before evaluating the evidence, we have to check on its reliability."

Greg rolled his eyes. "But that would mean redoing all the bookwork!"

"Some of it. Fortunately, we don't have to do this ourselves. That's what auditors are for."

"I remember them," Sue said. "When I was at work one day, I noticed a couple of people in a temporary office and was told they would be 'going over the books' for several weeks. I assumed they were putting together the annual report."

"Not writing it—that is normally done by the company. The auditors focus on the financial statements in the annual report, making independent checks to ascertain whether the information provided by management is factual and is presented in a standard, consistent manner."

"How do they do that without redoing the entire report?" Greg asked.

"By examining the books closely and taking judicious samples to verify the accounts. For example, they examine the inventory, do spot checks to see that income and expenses are appropriately recorded, check contractual obligations for accuracy and proper disclosure on the statements and dig further into specific areas when questions arise."

Standardization

"So auditors are supposed to keep management honest?" Sue asked.

"In part. They also make sure that the company's books and financial statements follow what are called Generally Accepted Accounting Principles, usually abbreviated as GAAP."

"To make sure everything is put into all those obscure accounting categories?" Greg grimaced.

"You'll be surprised at how quickly you'll become familiar with the most important terms. The key is standardization. For example, there is no way of ascertaining a company's profitability with a single figure."

"Can't you just subtract total costs from total sales?" Greg asked.

"Ultimately we do something like that, but a central question is what to count as 'costs.' Should one consider taxes as a cost? What about mortgage and loan payments? If we purchase major equipment and build a new plant to be used next year, should we count them as costs of the products we are selling this year? When we sell an item we made last year, do we count its cost what we paid to make it last year or what we will have to pay to replace it in inventory this year?"

"I can see where carrying items from year to year complicates things," Sue conceded. "Do the standard methods specify how such things are handled?"

"There is often more than one 'approved' way of reporting costs, sales and other items. Usually, however, a company has to pick one and stick to it. Otherwise, we could not compare the results from year to year in a meaningful way."

"Because we'd be comparing apples to oranges," Greg commented.

"Precisely. Furthermore, to get an idea of how well the company is running, we need to know more than its net profit and total assets. For example, we should know which goods were sold and what the inventory comprises—raw materials, work in process, and finished goods. Similarly, we need to know at least the major categories of costs, like those for manufacturing and selling the goods, and the general overhead costs, such as those for administration and interest payments."

"It feels like we're getting sucked into a quagmire of detail," Sue warned.

"We can't escape some of that," Holmes admitted, "but standardized statements help make this a manageable task. They contain enough information for us to piece together an accurate picture of the company and assure us that we know what is meant by each item in the statement.

"We'll be going over all these things one by one. Right now, we're just looking at the importance of standardized accounting methods. So let me conclude here by giving you a final thought: we also need to know how big a financial drain is caused by debts. A company with valuable assets could be in trouble because it is not operating efficiently; whereas another company, despite running well, might owe more that it can repay out of its normal operations."

The Auditors' Statement

Holmes paged through one of the reports for a moment, and then pointed to what looked like a letter at the beginning of the financial statement.

> To the Shareholders and the Board of Directors of the FerMon Corporation
>
> We have audited the accompanying balance sheet of your company as of December 31, 20__, and the related statements of income, capital accounts and retained earnings, and cash flows for the year then ended. These financial statements are the responsibility of your company's management. Our responsibility is to express an opinion on these financial statements based on our audit.
>
> We conducted our audit in accordance with auditing standards generally accepted in the United States of America. Those standards require that we plan and perform the audit to obtain reasonable assurance about whether the financial statements are free of material misstatement. An audit includes examining, on a test basis, evidence supporting the amounts and disclosures in the financial statements. An audit also includes assessing the accounting principles used and significant estimates made by management, as well as evaluating the overall financial statement presentation. We believe that our audit provides a reasonable basis for our opinion.
>
> In our opinion, the financial statements referred to above present fairly, in all material respects, the financial position of your company as of December 31, 20___, and the results of its operations and its cash flows for the year then ended, in conformity with accounting principles generally accepted in the United States of America.
>
> Signed: Ledger Domain Auditors, Ltd.

"The first two paragraphs sum up what we have already discussed," Holmes pointed out. "In this case, the auditors state that they have used sampling to verify the accuracy of the reported figures. The wording of the last paragraph is very important. In this case, it states that the auditors believe the report provides an accurate picture of the company's finances 'in all material respects.'

"Had they done only a limited amount of sampling, or none at all, they might have given a 'limited' opinion. For example, they might have limited their verifying opinion to only part of the information, like the Balance

Sheet, but not for the Income and Cash Flow Statements. If they had simply gone through the statement itself without doing any sampling, they might only have commented on the report's use of standard ways of presenting the information and on the accuracy of the computations, but not have offered any opinion on the information itself."

Requirements for Audited Reports

"I'm curious as to why a privately owned company would bother with all this," Greg said. "It's not like we're on the stock market."

"Actually, your parents never had audits," Holmes noted. "These started after I left. It's possible they are being done because of the trust. If Sue's rumor about loans is true, the lending bank would most likely have demanded audited statements to assess the credit-worthiness of the company.

"Audited statements would also be required if the company were to go public—start offering stock to the public. However, that wouldn't apply here since you own all the stock except for the few shares of voting stock held in trust."

"I never did understand how a few shares could control a company," Greg remarked.

"That's a way of passing on wealth without relinquishing control of a company," Holmes explained. "That's why you already receive all the dividends. When you reach the age specified in your parents' wills, you will receive control as well."

Sue appeared lost in thought for a moment, then hesitant, but she finally spoke. "Mr. Holmes, what has confused me the most about all this is the way we seem to jump around from one part of the statements to another. You keep telling us that no part is complete in itself and that we must constantly compare information in one section with that in another. Even then we might also have to look for further information outside of the statements. I sure wish we could just focus on one thing at a time."

"I'll try to do that. I just want you to be aware of the bigger picture. Too many people try to reduce everything to a narrow focus, like the 'bottom line,' and miss the really important things that are going on. As we go through the items in detail, both they and the connections will begin to make more sense."

CHAPTER 3

The Balance Sheet: Overview

Overview of the Financial Information

"Before we get down to particulars, let's look at the main parts of the complete financial statement," Holmes suggested. "We are not concerned with the front pages of large corporations' glossy annual reports to stockholders, which typically contain upbeat interpretations and graphics of the year's results, though they may contain useful information as well. Our concern here is with the more objective, financial, statements.

"As we have seen, an audited financial statement should have a letter from the auditors stating the degree to which they support the accuracy of the data and the way it is presented. In the statement itself, these are the major sections we'll look at in detail," he said as he wrote the following on a flip chart:

- **Balance Sheet:** What the company owns, how much of this is owed to others, and what is left over for the owners. Information on the balance sheet is for one particular point in time.

- **Income Statement:** What is sold minus expenses for a certain period of time.

- **Cash Flow:** How the financial transactions for the period affect the company's cash.

- **Financial Analyses:** Further calculations, called Ratio Analysis, to further determine the company's financial health."

Greg scratched his head. "Some of these things look similar to each other. For example, wouldn't cash flow be related to income?"

"Very good," Holmes said. "Yes, there are connections, and some financial statements may not present them all as distinct sections. The Financial Analysis is often not presented separately, but we can derive it from the data that is always supplied by making a few simple calculations. In any case, it is information we need to consider."

What Is Being Balanced?

"But, enough abstractions," Holmes continued. "It is time to look at the financial statement itself. Let's start with the Balance Sheet, because it gives a good overview of the company. To help understand the basics, let's focus on the statement for last year."

Balance Sheet: Last Year
(in thousands: $873 = $873,000)

ASSETS		LIABILITIES	
Cash & Equivalents	5,983	Notes Payable-Bank	18,563
Accounts Receivable-Trade	26,058	Current Portion LT Debt	873
Inventory	21,896	Accounts Payable-Trade	14,025
Prepaid Expenses	3,275	Other Accrued Expenses	5,003
CURRENT ASSETS	57,212	CURRENT LIABILITIES	38,464
Gross Fixed Assets	51,927	Long-Term Debt	8,731
Depreciation (-)	22,521	Deferred Taxes	271
NET FIXED ASSETS	29,406	TOTAL LIABILITIES	47,466
Intangible Assets	932	**CAPITAL**	
Other Noncurrent Assets	3,230	Capital Stock	8,218
		Retained Earnings	35,096
		TOTAL CAPITAL ·	43,314
TOTAL ASSETS	90,780	TOTAL	90,780

"I've always been confused by the idea of a Balance Sheet," Sue admitted. "What purpose is served by all the elaborate bookkeeping just to make two columns of numbers come out even?"

"I suppose the accountants would say that it is a method of making sure you've included everything and calculated it correctly," Holmes replied. "But it is also a way of representing the status of a company."

"There are all those funny terms again," Greg complained. "I'd rather have "nice" assets than "gross" ones."

Sue and Holmes supplied the obligatory groans.

"Seriously, though," Greg continued, "I don't see how it makes sense to put what the company owes in the same column with our owners' share, or 'Capital,' as it's called here."

"Also called the 'Shareholders' Equity.' Well, let's reduce this to the basic concept," Holmes suggested. He drew a figure on the flip chart:

Figure 1: The Basic Balance Sheet

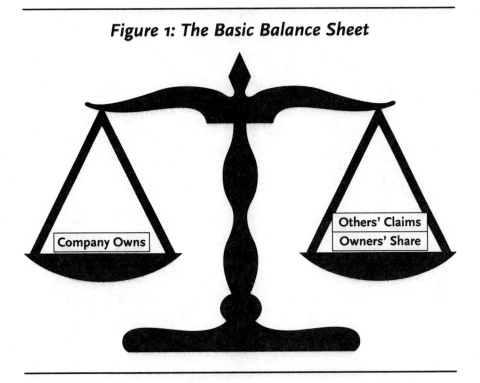

Pointing to the left side, he said, "We start with the assets that the company owns—whatever of value a company currently has in its possession. That includes its land, buildings, equipment, inventory, cash, investments, and the item called 'Accounts Receivable.' That last item is often simply referred to as the receivables; it means the money that is owed to it. Now, if the company were to convert all the assets to cash, how much would actually be yours?"

"Well, we'd have to pay off any bank loans," Sue replied, "and anyone else that was owed money."

"Exactly," Holmes said. "And that gives us one of the fundamental formulas:"

Assets – Liabilities = Owners' Equity

"Or, according to our illustration, take what is owed to others from what the company owns, and whatever is left is yours—what is commonly called the Shareholders' Equity or, more simply, the Capital."

"Another way of looking at it," Greg suggested, "is to consider everyone on the right side as having claims on what the company owns."

"Leveraging": Growing with Borrowed Money

After pondering the Balance Sheet and the illustration for a moment, Sue added, "So when a company makes money or increases in value, our share gets bigger, but when it loses, that comes out of our share?"

"That's generally correct for most transactions," Holmes said. "However, it does not hold true for loans used to expand its capabilities. When it buys a new plant with borrowed money, for example, we add the new plant to the left side (what the company owns) and the loan amount to the right side, under what is owed. Similarly, when a business sells part of its holdings, or Assets, to repay loans, we subtract what was sold from the Asset side and what was repaid from the 'owed,' or Liabilities, section on the other side.'"

"Well," Sue reasoned, "if something were sold off to repay a loan, we would own a bigger part of what was left."

"That's true. And if what was sold had not been doing too well, you would probably be better off. Remember, though, that borrowing money is a way of making a business larger and more profitable than you could make it by simply using your own money and the business's profits. It's the same principle as buying a bigger home with a mortgage. If you used your own money to buy a piece of property for $50,000 cash and it increased in value by twenty percent when you sold it, you would have earned $10,000 minus expenses, which would give you a 20% return on your original cash investment. With a mortgage, you might put that same $50,000 cash down on a $250,000 home: if it increased by twenty percent, to $300,000, when you sold it, you would have earned $50,000 minus your expenses, which would give you a 100% return on your original cash investment. This is called 'leveraging' because, like pushing on a lever, it is a way of producing greater results than you could by relying solely on your own strength."

"On the other hand," Greg pointed out, "you could also lose a lot more on the bigger property. If the properties lost twenty percent, you would lose the whole $50,000 on the $250,000 home. Would that be 'leveraging' one's losses?"

"That's also possible," Holmes conceded. "That is why, as we go through the financial statements, we will have to pay special attention to borrowed money."

"So if the budget-lamp division was bought with borrowed money," Sue noted, "it should be included in what the company owns, and the amount borrowed should balance it off on the other side, in what is owed."

"And," Greg added, "the company should show much better sales, though I don't see where that is listed in this Balance Sheet."

"Well, now we're getting a bit ahead of ourselves," Holmes cautioned. "In part, you should see growth in the owner's part of the balance sheet when you compare the statements over several years, including those before and after the acquisition. You would also want to see the amount owed being steadily paid off. And we'd have to look at the other parts of the statement as well. For now, let's just concentrate on the Balance Sheet."

Accrual: Accounting for Delayed Transactions

"Okay, I can see the value of recording long-term loans," Greg conceded. "But why can't we simplify matters by recording when we actually pay for something or are actually paid for our products? Why bother with all this complicated Accounts Receivable and Accounts Payable? Don't those amounts eventually go in and out the cash drawer? Why record these transactions twice?"

"Actually, some smaller companies do their accounting on a **cash basis**," Holmes said. "They recognize income and expenses only when actual cash changes hands, kind of like what most of us do with our personal finances. For example, the minute you charge something on your credit card, you start owing the money. However, you don't feel the impact until you write the check for your next credit-card bill. Likewise, **cash-basis companies don't recognize expense until they actually pay a bill, or recognize income until they actually receive the cash from the customer or client."**

"In a way," Greg conceded, "I can see how this method could get one in trouble, especially around the holidays or vacation times, when one can be shocked as the bills come pouring in."

"That's a good example," Holmes agreed. "Companies who use the accrual basis of accounting immediately record transactions as they occur. It's like setting an amount you will spend in a month and immediately subtracting every amount you charge to your credit card even though you haven't paid the bill yet."

"But doesn't recording income before you actually receive it cause you to pay real taxes on this theoretical money?" Sue objected.

"Yes, but this is usually offset by deducting expenses that haven't yet been paid in cash," Holmes pointed out.

"How does the Internal Revenue Service feel about that?" Sue asked.

"Actually, the IRS requires the vast majority of companies to use the accrual method because it gives a much more accurate picture of a company's income and expenses over a given period of time. It also gives us a more accurate accounting of what is owned and owed by the company at a given point in time."

"I was going to say that this sounds like 'a cruel' method of confusing us," Greg smiled, "but I'm beginning to see how it makes some sense."

CHAPTER 4

The Balance Sheet: Assets

Holmes flipped back to the previous year's Balance Sheet. "Okay, that is an overview of how the company holdings are balanced against what is owed and owned. We now need to examine the specific entries under these broad categories. This will help show both how the Balance Sheet works by itself and how it is tied into the other parts of the financial statement. Do you see the major categories of the company's assets?"

ASSETS	
Cash & Equivalents	5,983
Accounts Receivable-Trade	26,058
Inventory	21,896
Prepaid Expenses	3,275
CURRENT ASSETS	57,212
Gross Fixed Assets	51,927
Depreciation (-)	22,521
NET FIXED ASSETS	29,406
Intangible Assets	932
Other Noncurrent Assets	3,230
TOTAL ASSETS	90,780

Sue and Greg frowned at the chart. Then Sue said, "Well, there seem to be two main totals, 'Current' and 'Fixed.' I'm not sure where those final, smaller accounts fit."

"They're neither current nor fixed," Holmes smiled, "so let's begin by defining those two terms. Suppose you wanted to buy something very important and expensive: where would you begin looking for the money?"

Balance Sheet: Last Year
(in thousands: $873 = $873,000)

ASSETS		LIABILITIES	
Cash & Equivalents	5,983	Notes Payable-Bank	18,565
Accounts Receivable-Trade	26,058	Current Portion LT Debt	875
Inventory	21,896	Accounts Payable-Trade	14,025
Prepaid Expenses	3,275	Other Accrued Expenses	5,001
CURRENT ASSETS	57,212	CURRENT LIABILITIES	38,464
Gross Fixed Assets	51,927	Long-Term Debt	8,731
Depreciation (-)	22,521	Deferred Taxes	271
NET FIXED ASSETS	29,406	TOTAL LIABILITIES	47,466
Intangible Assets	952	CAPITAL	
Other Noncurrent Assets	3,250	Capital Stock	8,218
		Retained Earnings	35,096
		TOTAL CAPITAL	43,514
TOTAL ASSETS	90,780	TOTAL	90,780

"The logical place would be my checking and savings accounts," Greg replied.

"And if you still needed more money?"

"Well, I suppose I'd see whether I could sell some stocks or bonds," Sue said.

"Good! But what if that still wasn't enough?"

The cousins looked a bit uncomfortable. Then Greg said hesitatingly, "Well, if it was really important, I suppose I'd see about a loan."

"What about selling your car or your house?" Holmes asked.

"Well, I'd sure hate to do that," Sue said. "It would be hard to get around without a car, and finding a place to live would mean a lot of work and a loss of comfort."

"Besides," Greg added, "Selling those things, especially a home, would take quite a bit of time and, if we were in a hurry, could force us to lose money on them."

"Excellent!" Holmes exclaimed. "You have outlined most of the basic categories of a company's assets. The 'Current,' or 'liquid,' ones are cash or items that you can readily convert to cash within a year. The 'Fixed' ones are those that we need for our everyday operations; even if we decided to sell them, this would be a much slower process.

If you look at the 'Current' section, you will notice that the entries are listed in the order of how easily they can be converted into cash. First, there is cash itself and 'equivalents,' which are either investments that will come due within the year or things like money market accounts, stocks, and bonds that you regard as short-term investments that you can sell rather easily."

"I see," said Sue, "and Accounts Receivable is money that customers are supposed to pay within a short time—is that thirty days?"

"Usually," Holmes said, "though this varies for different industries and even from company to company. A significant amount of money owed for longer periods than a company has granted in the past can be a sign that it is dealing with riskier clients to boost sales."

Estimating the Inventory

"Then Inventory is what we make for sale, like the lamps, which might take more than thirty days to produce and sell," Greg added.

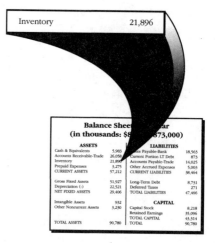

"It includes finished items," Holmes agreed, "but it also includes raw materials for making the lamps plus partially finished products, which accountants refer to, not surprisingly, as 'Work in Process.'"

"How on earth do you keep track of that?" Greg asked. "I hope someone doesn't have to follow each lamp down the assembly line."

"Heavens, no," Holmes laughed. "Even the stereotypical 'bean counters' aren't that compulsive. Still, Work in Process consumes raw materials, labor, and factory overhead—much of which is charged to Accounts Payable or taken from Cash before the product is finished and sold. So we need to balance these expenditures with the build-up of assets they have purchased and have on hand—in this case, Inventory. Furthermore, Inventory is a very important item to watch: tying up too much money in inventory is expensive and can be a sign of trouble."

"But, still, how do you know how much of these costs belong to each item that is sold?" Greg demanded.

"Some companies can actually assign costs to products as they are being made," Holmes said. "Other companies allocate estimated costs (called 'standard costs') to products based on their recent experience in making the products. They adjust these estimates to their actual costs at the end of an accounting period. When the actual cost is less than the estimated cost, the difference is called a 'positive variance'; when the actual cost is greater, the difference is called a 'negative variance.' At the end of each accounting period, these cost adjustments are allocated to the different inventory accounts (work in process and finished inventory). A total of the inventory on hand at the end of the period is then determined and entered on the Balance Sheet."

"So the value listed for Inventory is based upon the company's costs for making its products?" Sue summarized.

"Ideally. Remember, though, that financial statements are supposed to be based upon conservative estimates. In this case, if our current cost of replacing the inventory or the current market price is lower than our original costs, then we would have to use the lowest of these prices."

Prepaid Expenses

"I haven't a clue about what 'Prepaid Expenses' might be," Sue confessed.

"It covers goods and services for which you pay in advance, like insurance and advertising expenses that cover periods beyond the date on the Balance Sheet," Holmes explained.

"Or magazine subscriptions?" Sue asked.

"Well, perhaps some very expensive ones. The keys are that the period covered is rather extensive—not the shorter period typical of items in Accounts Receivable—and that the purchase involves a substantial amount of money that you cannot or do not want to write off immediately."

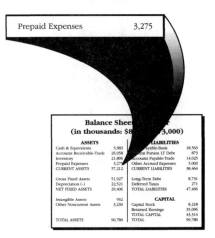

"But if you've already paid out the money, how can you consider this to be an asset?" Greg asked.

"Because we have the contractual right to receive services for those fees beyond the date of the Balance Sheet," Holmes replied. "For example, we usually pay our insurance premiums for a year in advance. Thus, at the time we prepare our Balance Sheet, we may have used up only a portion of the year's premium. What is left is considered 'prepaid' for the remainder of the policy year. Since we are entitled to the insurance coverage beyond the date on the Balance Sheet, the remaining premium is considered an asset that will be used up within the current year."

"One thing still puzzles me," Sue added. "How can this be considered a 'Current' or 'liquid' asset? Can we turn it into cash like we can the other items?"

"Sometimes. If a company were to move or go out of business, the insurance company might refund the money for the unused coverage or apply it towards the coverage of a new property. Note that Prepaid Expenses are at the bottom of the 'Current' list, which indicates they compose the least liquid item in this group."

Fixed Assets and Depreciation

"There's that 'gross' term again," Greg noted.

"Yes. There are Gross Sales, Gross Profits and other such items," Holmes said. "It means that some deductions must be made before we reach the 'Net' amount."

"Why not just make the deductions and show the real amount?" Greg asked.

"Because it is important to see how different kinds of costs affect the company," Holmes replied. "As we shall see in the Income Statement, it

| Gross Fixed Assets | 51,927 |
| Depreciation (-) | 22,521 |

Balance Sheet
(in thousands: $000)

ASSETS		LIABILITIES	
Cash & Equivalents	5,983	Bank	18,563
Accounts Receivable-Trade	26,058	Curr. portion LT Debt	873
Inventory	21,896	Accounts Payable-Trade	14,025
Prepaid Expenses	3,275	Accrued Expenses	5,003
CURRENT ASSETS	57,212	CURRENT LIABILITIES	38,464
Gross Fixed Assets	51,927	Long-Term Debt	8,731
Depreciation (-)	22,521	Deferred Taxes	271
NET FIXED ASSETS	29,406	TOTAL LIABILITIES	47,466
Intangible Assets	932	**CAPITAL**	
Other Noncurrent Assets	3,230	Capital Stock	8,218
		Retained Earnings	35,096
		TOTAL CAPITAL	43,314
TOTAL ASSETS	90,780	TOTAL	90,780

is important to separate the direct costs of making lamps, which include those for the raw materials, labor, and the plant, from expenses like administration and taxes. If we just had one lump sum of 'costs,' we could not tell where we were doing well and where we needed to make improvements."

"But surely that doesn't apply here," Sue objected. "Aren't Fixed Assets things like the buildings and equipment?"

"Yes, usually anything that costs a significant amount of money, lasts for a long time, and is used in the business is included in the Fixed Asset section of the Balance Sheet. These assets are often separated into Land, Buildings, Machinery and Equipment, and Furniture and Fixtures."

"Is that important?" Sue asked.

"It is when a company claims depreciation, which is almost always the case, because that provides a good tax deduction. Buildings generally last longer than equipment, so their depreciation schedule is stretched out over more years. The IRS does not allow depreciation on land, because land does not wear out like buildings and equipment."

"How do you determine the value of these things?" Greg asked. "If business properties are like homes, they might actually increase in value. Do you call in experts to give yearly appraisals?"

"Not usually," Holmes said. "Although Inventory is valued at the lower of cost or market, Gross Fixed Assets are valued at what they originally cost, which is known as the 'historical cost.' We then

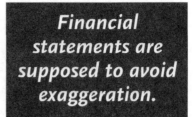

Financial statements are supposed to avoid exaggeration.

set up a Depreciation schedule, which gradually reduces the recorded book value of the building or equipment over a set number of years. The 'Depreciation' line shows the total amount deducted from the original cost of the asset, including the deduction for the current year. Subtracting the accumulated Depreciation from the 'Gross' amount gives us the 'Net Fixed Assets,' and this amount is what is included in the 'Total Assets.'"

"In other words, the 'Net Fixed Assets' might not be the actual value of the building and equipment if we sold them today?" Sue asked.

"That's true," Holmes conceded. "There are several reasons for handling them this way. One main reason is that financial statements are supposed to avoid exaggerations, so one is supposed to pick the most conservative way of evaluating assets. It is like buying a car or an appliance: you expect it to lose value as you use it. Using the historical cost for buildings and equipment is so common that using any other method might make the overall reliability of the financial statements suspect."

"But what if the buildings actually rise in value?" Greg asked.

"Then that would be a pleasant bonus, though one that would not bring in any real money unless we sold or refinanced the buildings and equipment. But FerMon is not really in the real estate business, the Balance Sheet is serving its primary purpose, which is to show how the company is doing in its main line of business—in FerMon's case, selling lamps."

"Okay, but where is this depreciation money going, into a special account to buy new buildings and equipment?" Sue asked.

"One could set up a special fund, but that would be not connected with the Depreciation line," Holmes answered. "In fact, larger businesses do not set up a specific account for this purpose because, in the long run, good businesses should earn a greater return by investing their extra money in their own activities than by putting it in a savings account. So the expectation is that a business will normally earn enough profits to replace its buildings and assets as the need arises.

"Whatever amount goes into the 'Accumulated Depreciation' account for the current year reduces both the Fixed Assets amount on the Balance Sheet and the taxable income on the year's tax return. However, no check is written for this, and it involves no reduction in cash or increase in debts. Because it is an expense, it will reduce our stated or 'book' income annually. We will look at this further when we consider Cash Flow."

Other Assets

"I'll bet those 'Intangible Assets' are hard to get a handle on," Greg quipped.

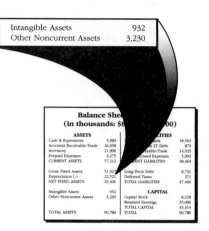

"They can be," Holmes admitted. "Nonetheless, there are many kinds, and some can be highly valuable, even the most valuable of some companies' holdings."

"Something you can't even touch?" Sue asked.

"Exactly, hence the term 'intangible.' Some of these items might include trademarks, patents, franchise rights, or copyrights. A special case is buying another company at a price higher than the value of its tangible assets."

"Why would one pay more?" Greg asked. "That doesn't sound like good business to me."

"Well, many a company has been purchased for its name, long-time customers, franchises, expert employees, copyrights, or patents," Holmes pointed out. "All of these intangible values are lumped under the term 'Good Will.' Accountants tend to be very conservative about assigning an exact value to this because even a patent that has generated large sales can suddenly lose value with the arrival of a new rival product. Nevertheless, those that significantly improve profits merit some mention on the Balance Sheet, and the extra money, or premium, paid for another company has to be accounted for as well. The premium, or Good Will, amount may be written off (amortized) over a number of years."

"What about that other mystery asset, 'Other Noncurrent'?" Greg asked.

"As you no doubt recall," Holmes answered, "we call those assets that will be used up or turned into cash within the year 'Current.' So these 'Noncurrent' ones are longer-term investments, such as notes receivable or investments in other companies that will not mature within the year, are not readily marketable, or are firmly designated as ones that the company will hold for more than a year."

CHAPTER 5

The Balance Sheet: Liabilities and Owners' Equity

Holmes pointed to the right side of the Balance Sheet. "Now we come to the debt, or liability, part, which is pretty straightforward."

"Sure," Sue noted, "it's what the company owes."

"Do you notice any similarities to the assets?" Holmes asked.

The cousins looked at the Balance Sheet for a moment, then Sue volunteered, "Do you mean the categories of 'Current' and 'Total'?"

"Right!" Greg added. "I suppose 'Current' means the same thing here—due within the year."

"You're both catching on," Holmes nodded. "Both Fixed Assets and the second group of liabilities are long-term, which means the company will take more than a year to use up the asset or pay off the debt. Since a com-

LIABILITIES	
Notes Payable-Bank	18,563
Current Portion LT Debt	873
Accounts Payable-Trade	14,025
Other Accrued Expenses	5,003
CURRENT LIABILITIES	38,464
Long-Term Debt	8,731
Deferred Taxes	271
TOTAL LIABILITIES	47,466

Balance Sheet: Last Year
(in thousands: $873 = $873,000)

ASSETS		LIABILITIES	
Cash & Equivalents	5,983	Notes Payable-Bank	18,563
Accounts Receivable-Trade	26,058	Current Portion LT Debt	873
Inventory	21,896	Accounts Payable-Trade	14,025
Prepaid Expenses	3,275	Other Accrued Expenses	5,003
CURRENT ASSETS	57,212	CURRENT LIABILITIES	58,464
Gross Fixed Assets	51,927	Long-Term Debt	8,731
Depreciation (-)	22,521	Deferred Taxes	271
NET FIXED ASSETS	29,406	TOTAL LIABILITIES	47,466
Intangible Assets	932	**CAPITAL**	
Other Noncurrent Assets	3,230	Capital Stock	8,218
		Retained Earnings	35,096
		TOTAL CAPITAL	43,314
TOTAL ASSETS	90,780	TOTAL	90,780

> *We can tell a lot about a company's overall financial health by comparing its total assets with its total liabilities.*

pany has to use assets to pay off its debts, we can tell a lot about a company's overall financial health by comparing its total assets with its total liabilities. We can also detect a short-term cash-flow problem by calculating whether its current assets are sufficient to cover its current liabilities. But let's start by looking at the various types of Current

Liabilities.

"Notes Payable, as you can see, is bank loans."

"But I thought bank loans were usually for big, long-term projects," Sue said.

"Not necessarily," Holmes replied. "Short-term means loans that will be paid in full within a year. Sometimes a company needs cash to buy raw materials to make finished goods. When the goods are sold and the account receivable from the sale is collected, the cash then goes to pay off the loan. Such loans are often referred to as 'self-liquidating.'"

"That sounds like a hand-to-mouth existence to me," Greg observed.

"It could be," Holmes agreed. "However, it could be a sign of more positive events as well, such as an unusually large number of new orders or the company's having tied its cash up in a profitable expansion program. We'll get a better idea of what's going on when we look at the Income Statement and the Cash Flow."

"What is the 'Current Portion LT Debt'?" Greg asked.

"The 'LT' stands for 'long-term,' which means debts that do not need to be repaid in full for over a year," Holmes explained. "As with a mortgage or car loan, part of a long-term loan is paid back every year. The 'Current Portion' represents the next twelve months of payments. Every year when the Balance Sheet is drawn up, the amount due in the coming year is subtracted from the 'Long Term Debt' and placed on this 'Current Portion' line, because it has become, in effect, a current debt."

"Why is there an 'Accounts Payable–Trade' but no other listing of Accounts Payable?" Sue asked.

"Good eye!" Holmes nodded. "This listing covers what the company owes for its purchases, such as raw materials. It is sort of the counterpart to Accounts Receivable, which is what the customers owe for what they bought from the company. The other category for short-term debts is, appropriately, 'Other Accrued Expenses.' Do you remember what 'accrued' means?"

"Sure," Greg answered. "Something that's immediately entered as an asset or a debt before any money exchanges hands."

"Correct. So, in a way, the Other Accrued Expenses constitute the other category of Accounts Payable."

"So what might be included in 'Other Accounts Payable'?" Greg asked.

"They include things like pay owed to the employees, money from payroll deductions, and income taxes that will have to be paid during the coming year." Holmes answered.

"I thought employees were paid regularly," Sue objected.

"They are. However, they are usually paid for work already completed, which means that there is some delay between the time when they earn the money and when they actually receive it. The length of time varies from company to company, of course, but one week is very common; when you multiply that by hundreds of employees, the amount of money is considerable."

"What about the payroll deductions?" Sue asked.

"Again, on every payday, the company sets aside federal and state taxes, Social Security taxes, insurance and retirement payments, and so on, but it may not have to actually pay out this money for weeks or even months. Since the company has to pay these bills within twelve months, they are classified as 'current' liabilities."

"Well, if you are accounting for taxes here, then what is the 'Deferred Taxes' line a little further down?" Greg demanded.

"This gets a bit complicated," Holmes warned. "Sometimes the government allows companies to use different accounting methods for tax purposes than it uses for its company books. This results in a delay in paying certain taxes for a specified period of time. This may require the company to keep a second accounting record to reflect the tax treatment of the affected transactions. However, the company also has to keep a set of accounting records that more accurately represent the shareholder interests. This set shows the taxes that would normally be paid by the end of the year without the special delay. The 'Deferred Taxes' line on the normal accounting record corrects the difference between the two records by telling the amount of the taxes that have been 'deferred'—that is, that are not due immediately but will be due some time in the future."

Capital – The Owners' Share

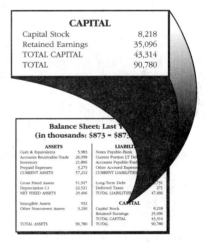

"Here's Greg's favorite part," Sue teased.

"Well, if you don't like it, you can give me your share," Greg quipped.

"Oh, I don't *dislike* it," Sue responded.

"Okay," Holmes intervened. "This part requires a little more explanation than Liabilities."

"Yeah," Greg agreed. "To begin with, why is it called 'Capital' instead of 'Assets'?"

"We use the term 'assets' for the actual things owned by the company, which are listed on the left side of the Balance Sheet," Holmes explained. "The owners supplied the original money, or capital, to start up the company, and this is supplemented in publicly traded companies by selling additional stock. Capital also comprises profits left in the company over the years for further growth."

"If the common stock represents our ownership, then why doesn't it include all of what our company is worth?" Sue asked.

"Because a financial statement reflects historic costs, or Book Value and is not meant to reflect the market value of assets or the company's stock," Holmes explained. "The Capital section of the Balance Sheet clearly differentiates between the shareholders' original investment in the Common Stock of the company and the earnings that have been reinvested back in the company over time. In a well-established company, the Capital Stock should be a relatively small part of the Total Capital. This is the final part of the Balance Sheet equation:

Assets – Liabilities = Total Capital

"The 'Total Capital' may also be referred to as 'Net Worth' or 'Shareholders' Equity.' It represents what would be left over for the owners if all the company's assets were liquidated for one hundred cents on the dollar and all the liabilities were paid in full."

Retained Earnings

"Well, by default, then, 'Retained Earnings' should be what the company has earned through the years," Greg ventured.

"It is what the company has earned, but not all of it," Holmes replied. "Don't forget all the dividends you and your families have received through the years. If you took all the profits as dividends, there would be no Retained Earnings, and the company would never grow or even keep up with inflation. That's why some, usually most, profits are 'retained' and invested in the company. In some publicly traded companies (those with stock that is available for sale to the public), little or none of the profits is given as dividends to the shareholders. The rationale is that reinvesting the money in the company will raise the value of the stock and ultimately give the shareholders more money than they would have received in dividends."

"So we have to add together Capital Stock and Retained Earnings to get Total Capital, which means how much money our ownership is worth," Sue concluded.

"Well," Holmes hesitated, "that's the general theory. You realize, of course, that most of what you own is not cash in the bank but fixed assets, which you could not turn into cash without selling part or all of the company. You may also recall that the historical costs of the fixed assets does not necessarily show what they would bring if they were put up for sale. In addition, the 'book value' does not reflect any premiums a potential buyer might be willing to pay for our company's 'good will'—such things as intellectual capital, location, and customer loyalty. The book value will also not include the current market values for our fixed assets such as real estate or equipment."

"If that's so, then what is the value of the Balance Sheet?" Greg asked.

"First of all, it gives us a reasonable snapshot of complex and dynamic business dealings," Holmes answered. "Second, it gives us a consistent picture of our assets, liabilities, and capital based on generally accepted accounting principles so that, when we compare the reports from year to year or our company's reports with those of other companies in the industry, we can compare apples with apples. Comparing the reports from consecutive years is especially important, because the changes from year to year give us a pretty good idea of the company's health: whether it is growing, stagnating, or losing ground. So let us turn to the full Balance Sheet, which shows the figures for the past five years."

CHAPTER 6

The Balance Sheet: Five-Year Comparisons

Holmes spread out the five-year Balance Sheet on the table:

Balance Sheet: Five-Year
(in thousands: $873 = $873,000)

ASSETS	Year 1	Year 2	Year 3	Year 4	Year 5
Cash & Equivalents	4,242	5,129	6,386	6,092	5,983
Accounts Receivable-Trade	17,033	19,591	23,860	25,890	26,058
Inventory	13,626	16,120	18,715	21,232	21,896
Prepaid Expenses	1,543	1,735	2,767	3,046	3,275
CURRENT ASSETS	36,444	42,575	51,728	56,260	57,212
Gross Fixed Assets	38,089	44,287	48,660	49,970	51,927
Depreciation (-)	12,148	14,577	17,261	19,870	22,521
NET FIXED ASSETS	25,941	29,710	31,399	30,100	29,406
Intangible Assets	913	872	851	860	932
Other Noncurrent Assets	977	3,972	4,719	2,665	3,230
TOTAL ASSETS	64,275	77,129	88,697	89,885	90,780
LIABILITIES					
Notes Payable-Bank	6,413	12,234	17,978	18,201	18,563
Current Portion LT Debt	1,066	1,185	1,096	943	873
Accounts Payable-Trade	8,066	9,780	12,223	13,348	14,025
Other Accrued Expenses	4,488	4,820	4,886	5,044	5,003
CURRENT LIABILITIES	20,033	28,019	36,183	37,536	38,464
Long-Term Debt	10,663	11,847	10,963	9,433	8,731
Deferred Taxes	71	113	142	179	271
TOTAL LIABILITIES	30,767	39,979	47,288	47,148	47,466
CAPITAL					
Capital Stock	8,218	8,218	8,218	8,218	8,218
Retained Earnings	25,290	28,932	33,191	34,519	35,096
TOTAL CAPITAL	33,508	37,150	41,409	42,737	43,314
TOTAL	64,275	77,129	88,697	89,885	90,780

"Earlier I compared the Balance Sheet with a snapshot at a certain point in time. Like a bank or credit card statement, it tells you how much you have in an account or owe on your account on a particular day. By the time you receive the statement, dramatic changes could have occurred."

"You mean we could have deposited a considerable amount of money or charged something big," Sue said.

"Yes. If I wanted to obtain an accurate picture of your spending and saving habits, I would want to see the statements from a number of months if not years. Then I would have a better idea of how much you normally maintain in savings or charge to your card. Just a single statement might show an unusually high or low amount of savings or charges."

"Like around the holidays," Sue noted.

"Exactly. Now, a motion picture comprises many snapshots: when they are shown in rapid succession, we see motion. In the same way, by looking at the reports for several years, we begin to sense where the company is moving.

"As we go through the financial statements, also keep in mind the importance of relating particular numbers to others in the statement, because no number in itself provides conclusive information. It's sort of like the connect-the-dots pictures we all worked as kids."

"I remember those," Greg said. "They had scattered dots with numbers; only when you drew lines between the right numbers could you see the overall picture."

"That's a pretty good picture of what I'm saying," Holmes agreed. "Above all, we want to avoid 'bottom line disease,' the malady of those who skip past the Balance Sheet to find the 'Net Profit' on the Income Statement and think they have now found the only important indicator of a company's health."

Assessing the Assets

"The first account I like to look at on the Balance Sheet is 'Total Assets.' As we can see, FerMon has grown from about $64 million in total assets to over $90 million in the last five years, a gain of about $26.5 million."

"That sounds good," Greg said.

"Well, I wonder," Sue said thoughtfully. "If what I heard about heavy borrowings and diminishing profits, then it could be that our increased assets have actually weakened the company."

"Excellent observation, Sue," Holmes exclaimed. "You have pointed out two of the additional facts we have to look at: how the increased assets were financed, and how well they are performing. First, though, let's finish looking at the assets.

"To continue looking at the bigger picture, where has most of this growth occurred?" Holmes asked.

After the cousins had studied the sheet for a few moments, Greg said, "It looks like Current Assets have grown by about $21 million, whereas Fixed

Assets have only grown by about $3.5 million."

"Yes," Sue agreed, "and most of the increase in Current Assets has come through a $9 million increase in Accounts Receivable and an $8 million increase in Inventory. That sounds like a lot of people suddenly owe us money, and that the stuff in inventory is not selling."

"But it could also mean we're selling more," Greg countered. "If we expanded and got more customers, the Accounts Receivable would naturally increase with everything else, and we'd have to keep more lamps in inventory to handle more orders."

ASSETS	Year 1	Year 2	Year 3	Year 4	Year 4
Cash & Equivalents	4,242	5,129	6,386	6,092	5,983
Accounts Receivable-Trade	17,033	19,591	23,860	25,890	26,058
Inventory	13,626	16,120	18,715	21,232	21,896
Prepaid Expenses	1,543	1,735	2,767	3,046	3,275
CURRENT ASSETS	36,444	42,575	51,728	56,260	57,212
Gross Fixed Assets	38,089	44,287	48,660	49,970	51,927
Depreciation (-)	12,148	14,577	17,261	19,870	22,521
NET FIXED ASSETS	25,941	29,710	31,399	30,100	29,406
Intangible Assets	913	872	851	860	932
Other Noncurrent Assets	977	3,972	4,719	2,665	3,230
TOTAL ASSETS	64,275	77,129	88,697	89,885	90,780

Balance Sheet: Five-Year
(in thousands: $873 = $873,0

"If we confine our information to these few lines, either of you could be right," Holmes pointed out. "That's why we have to look further.

"Let's finish with the details of the Current Assets, where most of the growth has come. As Sue pointed out, most of this growth has been in Inventory and Accounts Receivable. Cash has averaged about $6 million over the past three years, and there was still a substantial amount, about $4.2 million, in the first year reported on this sheet, so this has been a fairly constant item."

"That seems like a lot of money to keep on hand," Greg said.

"There are different philosophies on this," Holmes said. "Many companies keep a minimum amount of cash on hand and borrow from the bank when they need more. They believe this keeps their money working in the most profitable way. Others keep larger amounts of cash on hand to meet normal needs during the year so they don't have to borrow money from a bank. They like to avoid short-term cash shortages or expensive short-term loans during sudden downturns in business. Beyond determining whether we have enough cash on hand to pay our regular bills, the important thing to know is what strategy the management uses in managing cash and why."

"I'm a little curious about the steady increase in Prepaid Expenses," Sue noted, "even though it is a relatively small amount."

"Our Fixed Assets went up by $14 million, so the insurance probably went up, too," Greg pointed out.

"No doubt that's part of it," Holmes agreed. "However, the Prepaid Expenses more than doubled, while the Gross Assets went up by only about a third, and the Net Fixed Assets increased by only 13 percent. To figure out what happened here requires more detailed information than a Balance Sheet supplies. However, the Prepaid Expenses item involves a much smaller amount than the other increases, so we should concentrate on them first.

"Now that we are looking at this section, note that $10 million of the $14 million jump in Gross Fixed Assets came during Years Two and Three. During the five years that Gross Fixed Assets increased by $14 million, the Accumulated Depreciation only increased by about $10 million. Generally, we like to see annual depreciation expenses at least equal to increases in Fixed Assets. In this case, the company invested about forty percent more than the depreciation amount. I would guess that this major investment was largely spent on the purchase and equipping of the branch manufacturing location that produces the lower-cost line of lamps that Sue talked about earlier."

"That timing sounds about right," Sue noted. "But if we just added a new plant, why have Net Fixed Assets gone down recently?"

"Presumably," Holmes replied, "after buying the new manufacturing facility, the company has restricted additional investment to replacing worn-out equipment in all its facilities or new equipment that can do a better job than the older equipment. In the meantime, it has continued subtracting depreciation from the original cost. In fact, the significant jump in Depreciation plus the declining amounts in Years Four and Five suggest that the company has taken accelerated depreciation for the new plant. That's where one takes larger amounts of depreciation in the early years of a fixed assets life.

"There's one other aspect of this worth noting. In Year One, the accumulated Depreciation was less than one-third the amount of the Gross Fixed Assets; by Year Five, the Depreciation had become almost one-half the size of the remaining book value of the Fixed Assets despite the purchase of the new plant. This means that the remaining assets are getting more fully depreciated and could indicate aging assets or accelerated depreciation methods."

"How can we tell whether this is the case?" Greg asked.

"We would need to look at the ages of the assets and their condition—something the financial statements won't tell us. We can also look at the Income Statement for indications of increasing maintenance costs or decreasing efficiency in the plant," Holmes answered.

"I see that Intangible Assets has remained pretty steady, but Other Noncurrent Assets has varied quite a bit and is currently about $2.5 million higher than it was in Year One," Sue noted.

"That might be worth looking into—another item not fully listed on the statement," Holmes agreed. "However, right now we should concentrate on the $17 million increase in Current Assets and on how these increases are accounted for under Liabilities and Equity."

Liabilities

"Starting again with the big picture, we see that the Total Liabilities have increased by $17 million over the past five years, and Total Capital has risen by $10 million," Holmes pointed out. "That means that almost two-thirds of the growth in assets has been financed by loans. In the Equity section, the Capital Stock remains the same, so the remaining third of the financing has come from Retained Earnings, or the owners' profits."

LIABILITIES					
Notes Payable-Bank	6,413	12,234	17,978	18,201	18,563
Current Portion LT Debt	1,066	1,185	1,096	943	873
Accounts Payable-Trade	8,066	9,780	12,223	13,348	14,025
Other Accrued Expenses	4,488	4,820	4,886	5,044	5,003
CURRENT LIABILITIES	20,033	28,019	36,183	37,536	38,464
Long-Term Debt	10,663	11,847	10,963	9,433	8,731
Deferred Taxes	71	113	142	179	271
TOTAL LIABILITIES	30,767	39,979	47,288	47,148	47,466

"Well, if it came from there, then how come that amount hasn't gone down?" Greg asked.

"Remember," Holmes said, "Retained Earnings, or profits, do not mean there is cash in the bank. It is related to the company's assets, which could be anything from cash to plants and equipment. If the company took, say, $2 million from cash and bought $2 million worth of equipment, the Total Assets would remain the same, and the Retained earnings would not be affected."

"This reliance on borrowing would seem to corroborate what the employees told me about big debts," Sue noted.

"Well, as I said earlier, borrowing can be a way of 'leveraging' other people's money into more rapid growth," Holmes said. "The main concern about borrowing is that you make more money with the new plant than it costs you to pay off the loan.

"One disturbing number that jumps out at me is that the Current Liabilities, or the short-term debts due within the year, have risen by about $18.5 million. Though the Long-Term Debt rose slightly at the time of the expansion, overall it has actually gone down by $2 million. The short-term loans from banks have risen every year, increasing by over $12 million. In effect, all of the financing from non-owners that was used for our new Fixed Assets involve obligations maturing in less than one year."

"Gee, that sounds like a person getting buried in credit-card debts," Greg commented. "Sue, it's beginning to look like you were right to drag me here."

"I'd rather be wrong in this case," Sue replied. "Here's another figure that looks disturbing: the rise in Accounts Payable from $8 million to $14 million. It looks like there is a problem paying bills."

"Yes. That and the rise in short-term loans may suggest a cash-flow problem," Holmes said. "There is another calculation we can do for liquidity:

there are $57 million in Current Assets for paying off $38 million in Current Liabilities. That is a ratio of only 1.5 to 1 between Current Assets and Current Liabilities. Generally we would like to see a 2-to-1 ratio to allow some cushion in case we have to liquidate current assets to pay current liabilities."

"Well, at least it sounds like there's enough to pay the bills for the time being," Greg remarked.

"Perhaps," Holmes said thoughtfully. "Note, though, that most of the Current Assets amount, about $48 million, is tied up in Accounts Receivable and Inventory."

"Oh, yeah," Greg conceded. "And we saw how both of these have been growing, which could mean that the chances are increasing that we might not collect all that is owed to us or be unable to sell all that is in Inventory. So things could be even worse than they look."

"Let's not jump to conclusions," Holmes cautioned. "We have found reason to look further but may find from the Income Statement that profitability is improving, and from the Cash Flow Statement that liquidity is improving as well. Before going on to the Income Statement, let's summarize our major findings on the five-year Balance Sheet." He wrote on the flip chart:

- Investment in the company (Total Assets) grew by $26.5 million.

- Outsiders' investments (Total Liabilities) increased by $16.5 million, while the owners' investment (Capital) increased by $10 million.

- The Current Assets (Working Capital investments) grew by $21 million, while the Net Fixed Assets grew by about $3.5 million (after subtracting Depreciation).

- Our longer-term assets increased overall by about $3.5 million (counting $15 for a new plant in Years Two and Three, and subtracting accumulated Depreciation).

- Our growth in assets was financed primarily by short-term debt (up $18.5 million), while our long-term obligations went down by $2 million.

- Most of the increase in Current Assets, $17 million, is in Accounts Receivable and Inventory.

- Accounts Payable has risen by $9 million.

CHAPTER 7

The Income Statement

"Now that we have seen where the company has been putting money into the business and how it has financed that investment, we need to find out how profitably the management is using all the assets, how fast the company is growing and whether the growth is being supported by the operating profits of the company," Holmes said. "The answers to these questions can be found in the Income Statement, which is sometimes referred to as the Profit and Loss Statement (P&L)."

He turned to the Income Statement in the annual report and commented: "As we did with the Balance Sheet, we will focus on the returns for last year in order to see how this statement works. Then we will compare the numbers for the past five years to determine the longer-term trends."

Dynamic View

"Unlike the Balance Sheet, which reflects accounts on a particular day, the Income Statement contains the revenues and expenses for a significantly longer period of time, in this case a year, so it provides us with a more dynamic picture," Holmes continued. "Specifically, the difference between the revenues and expenses incurred during this longer period results in either a net profit or a net loss for that period."

After looking at the statement for a few moments, Greg objected, "It looks to me as though this statement, like the Balance Sheet, has a definite date. So what makes the Income Statement more dynamic?"

"In the Balance Sheet," Holmes explained, "we see, for example, how much cash or inventory is on hand on a particular day. However, we do not see how much cash and or how many materials have changed hands in the course of the year. Similarly, the Balance Sheet shows us the Retained Earnings for that date but gives us no idea how that amount has varied throughout the year or how many sales were required to produce it."

"I thought looking at the five-year Balance Sheet provided a more dynamic picture," Greg noted.

"True," Holmes conceded. "But that still leaves us at the big-picture level: how much the company is growing overall, how its overall debts compare with its net worth and owners' equity, and so on. As we have seen, this is valuable information, but it does not show us how the company is operating. What the Income Statement shows us is how the company made its profits or suffered its losses—how many sales there were and how much expenses reduced profits each year. Note what the final figure on this statement is."

"Ending Retained Earnings," Sue observed. "Is this where the 'Retained Earnings' line on the Balance Sheet comes from?"

"Actually, both entries come from the books," Holmes explained. "The Balance Sheet, the Income Statement, and the Cash Flow Statement are all computed separately. However, the overlapping amounts, like 'Retained Earnings' on the Balance Sheet and the Income Statement, and 'Cash' on the Balance Sheet and the Cash Flow Statement, have to reconcile or there is an error somewhere. This is called 'reconciling' the statements."

"So we could call the Income Statement the story behind Retained Earnings, and the Cash Flow Statement the story behind the cash amount," Greg concluded.

The Major Calculations

"Notice that the major calculations begin with Sales, which produce most of a manufacturing company's income," Holmes pointed out.

"That makes sense, since we are

SALES in thousands	
Gross Sales	159,226
Returns and Allowances	7,399
Discounts	3,847
Net Sales	147,980
COST OF SALES	
Material	53,569
Labor	27,524
Depreciation	1,820
Other Manufacturing Overhead	17,210
Total Cost of Sales	100,123
Gross Profit	47,857
EXPENSES	
Salary Payroll	13,614
Hourly Payroll	5,179
Payroll Taxes	2,819
Benefits	1,924
Research & Development	1,776
Warranty	1,317
Depreciation	829
Scrap	4,380
Supplies (Office & Operating)	252
Repair & Maintenance	1,243
Advertising & Marketing	89
Telephone	740
Utilities	1,273
Insurance	2,649
Taxes (Real Estate, etc.)	577
Bad Debts	2,323
Other	422
TOTAL	41,406
Operating Income	6,451
Other Income & Expenses	
Interest Expenses	4,587
Other Income (Expenses)	444
Net Income Before Tax	2,308
Income Taxes	
Net Income After Tax	2,308
Beginning Retained Earnings	34,519
Less: Tax Dividends	958
Other	773
Ending Retained Earnings	35,096

in the business of making lamps to sell," Greg agreed. "What other income would there be?"

"Towards the bottom, you see Other Income," Holmes said, pointing.

"That takes care of miscellaneous forms of income like gains on the sale of assets and interest from investments outside the company."

"Like bank accounts?" Sue asked.

"Yes, or investments in bonds or even other companies," Holmes replied. "We put that later in the statement because we are more interested in the company's primary business."

"Okay, but why is there a division between 'Costs of Sales' and 'Expenses'? Why not lump all expenditures together?" Greg asked.

"Because we want to see how efficient we are at making lamps and how much the other company overhead is costing us," Holmes replied. "Suppose the board declared that declining profits meant we had to close one of the plants and buy lamps from other suppliers?"

"I'd try to fight that," Sue declared.

"So would I," Greg agreed. "But I see your point, Mr. Holmes. By separating the costs of making the lamps from other expenses, we could see whether the problem lay in our manufacturing plants or in other areas."

"And," Sue put in, "if the problem lay elsewhere, like in administrative expenses, going to a different supplier would not help. In a way, figuring just what it costs to make a lamp lets us think of it as a purchase from the factory, which we can compare with the cost of buying a lamp from an outside supplier."

Holmes nodded his agreement. "So, then, subtracting the cost of goods sold from the sales income gives us the Gross Profit."

"I remember 'gross,'" Greg smiled. "It means we have to make further subtractions to arrive at the final, or 'net,' figure. Obviously, we have to pay all the expenses before we can declare a real profit."

"That's true," Holmes agreed. "However, the Gross Profit is a very important number in itself. For example, we can divide it by the Net Sales to get the Gross Margin. Last year, that would be $47,857,000 divided by $147,980,000, which gives us 32 percent. In other words, for every dollar we receive for our lamps, 68 cents pays for the factory expenses, and 32 cents is our Gross Profit, from which we pay our other expenses and derive our net profit."

Sue frowned at the statement for a moment. "I understand the next step, subtracting the Operating Expenses, which seems to include the administration, office expenses, and sales expenses. Is this our 'bottom line'?"

"Not quite," Holmes replied. "Even after figuring in the 'Other Income and Expenses' items, which are secondary to the primary, manufacturing, business, we still have to deduct Income Taxes."

"Why?" Greg demanded. "I mean, I know you have to pay the taxes, but why should they count against the company's profit? When people talk about their salaries, they mean what they earn before paying taxes."

"But don't you figure your after-taxes income when you decide how much you can afford for mortgage or car payments, vacations, and so forth?"

"Well, sure," Greg conceded.

"Well, companies have to figure out what money they actually have for paying off debts, distributing dividends, and reinvesting in themselves," Holmes argued. "So one can think of 'Net Income after Tax' as the real 'bottom line,' the money the company actually has to work with."

Net Sales

"Now that we have gone over the big picture, let's go back and pick up some of the more significant details," Holmes suggested. "We can start with Greg's favorites, Gross and Net."

"My turn," interrupted Sue. "I would imagine that Gross Sales are every confirmed order—or would that be every shipped order?"

"Every shipped order, because that's when the company is either immediately paid in cash or, far more commonly, enters the order into its Accounts Receivable ledger. We don't count orders that are canceled before they are shipped."

"Okay," Sue continued. "Then I gather that the 'Returns' part refers to items that the customers ship back."

Holmes nodded.

"But aren't the customers a little old to be given allowances?" Greg quipped.

"I'd say we are making allowances for you right now," Sue retorted.

"Technically, 'Allowances' takes in reduced billing for things like damaged or lost items we shipped. In practice, we can consider the entire phrase 'Returns and Allowances' to mean merchandise returned by the customers," Holmes explained. "Generally, returns are due to defects in the products, an error on the order, or some other problem. So an unusually large number here could signal quality problems."

"I don't understand the 'Discount' line," Greg said. "If we sell lamps at a lower price, why don't we record that amount in the first place?"

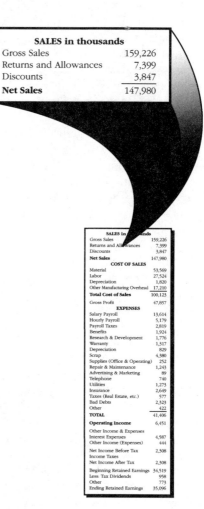

SALES in thousands	
Gross Sales	159,226
Returns and Allowances	7,399
Discounts	3,847
Net Sales	147,980

SALES in thousands	
Gross Sales	159,226
Returns and Allowances	7,399
Discounts	3,847
Net Sales	147,980
COST OF SALES	
Material	53,569
Labor	27,524
Depreciation	1,820
Other Manufacturing Overhead	17,210
Total Cost of Sales	100,123
Gross Profit	47,857
EXPENSES	
Salary Payroll	13,614
Hourly Payroll	5,179
Payroll Taxes	2,819
Benefits	1,924
Research & Development	1,776
Warranty	1,317
Depreciation	829
Scrap	4,380
Supplies (Office & Operating)	252
Repair & Maintenance	1,243
Advertising & Marketing	89
Telephone	740
Utilities	1,273
Insurance	2,649
Taxes (Real Estate, etc.)	577
Bad Debts	2,323
Other	422
TOTAL	41,406
Operating Income	6,451
Other Income & Expenses	
Interest Expenses	4,587
Other Income (Expenses)	444
Net Income Before Tax	2,308
Income Taxes	
Net Income After Tax	2,308
Beginning Retained Earnings	34,519
Less: Tax Dividends	958
Other	773
Ending Retained Earnings	35,096

"We do for an agreed-upon price," Holmes replied. "However, many deductions are granted after the sale. For example, many companies offer a two-percent deduction if a customer pays within ten days, or net price for payment within 30 days. So the two-percent deduction would come when the customer actually paid the bill, which could be ten days after the original sale was recorded in the Accounts Receivable ledger. Some companies, like automobile manufacturers, offer a series of paybacks throughout the year for dealers who end up buying larger quantities of vehicles."

Cost of Sales

"As I look at this section, I don't see anything for advertising or sales commissions," Sue noted.

COST OF SALES	
Material	53,569
Labor	27,524
Depreciation	1,820
Other Manufacturing Overhead	17,210
Total Cost of Sales	100,123

"Actually, 'Cost of Sales' refers to manufacturing costs, not selling costs," Holmes answered. "Sometimes this entry is more accurately labeled the 'Cost of Goods Sold.' Keeping this in mind, can you figure out the individual items in this list?"

"Well, I assume the 'Material' means the raw materials used to make the lamps, and the 'Labor' means the wages paid to those who make the lamps," Greg answered.

"Right," Holmes agreed. "The direct labor and the raw materials are the costs that directly apply to the making of lamps."

"So the 'Other Manufacturing Overhead' is indirect costs?" Sue asked.

"Well, not too indirect. That entry includes everything else needed to keep the factories running, including the salaries of the supervisors, electricity, maintenance, and depreciation. These factory overhead items all contribute to the production of lamps, but one cannot precisely determine how much of these general costs apply to an individual lamp in the same way one can figure out how many materials or hours of assembly work are involved."

"But what about Depreciation?" Greg asked. "I see that also appears in the operating expenses."

"The general principle is that depreciation on factories and their equipment is counted as a production cost, ultimately a part of the Cost of Goods Sold, and depreciation on administrative buildings and their equipment is counted as an administrative cost," Holmes replied.

"But our administration shares one of the factory buildings," Sue objected. "And, now that I think of it, they must share a lot of services, like telephone and electricity."

"True," Holmes conceded. "There are many ways of working this out. Some companies figure out how many square feet the administration uses and how many the factory uses and split the costs and depreciation proportionately. Others use more sophisticated methods of estimating what each uses. For example, one might expect a factory with its higher ceilings and heavier machinery to use more electricity, and the administrative offices to use more telephone service. We can leave these details to the accountants."

Calculating the Inventory

Greg was lost in thought. Finally he shook his head and pointed to the Cost of Sales section. "I'm still a little confused about how these costs relate to actual sales. I would expect some sales to use items that were in the inventory at the beginning of the year, and for some items made during this year to be in the inventory at the end of the year. So how can we charge all of this year's work, and just this year's work, to this year's sales?"

"You're absolutely right," Holmes answered. "There is an overlap at each end, and, by definition, the 'Cost of Goods Sold' applies only to merchandise that has actually been sold and shipped. The unsold finished products, unused raw materials, and the Work in Process compose the Ending Inventory."

"Well, then," Sue asked, "what do these items like 'Materials' and 'Labor' mean, if not the expenditures made during the past year?"

"Ultimately, they represent the amounts used in the goods actually sold," Holmes replied. "But let's work our way towards this. Suppose FerMon made only a single type of lamp. To figure the value of the lamps we had sold from the inventory, we would start with the dollar value of the inventory at the beginning of the year and add to that the amount we spent adding to it during the year. Finally, we would subtract the dollar value still in inventory at the end of the year, and that would give us the value of what we had sold during the year."

"Now that seems like a laborious way of doing things," Greg objected. "Why can't we just keep track of how much we sold?"

"Well, of course, the accountants do," Holmes answered. "But, remember, the prices of materials, labor, and the factory overhead can change significantly during the year, so we need to account for those changes in some way. So here is the general way of calculating these costs:"

```
     Beginning Inventory
  +  Raw Materials Purchased
  +  Direct labor
  +  Factory Overhead
  -  Ending Inventory
     Cost of Goods Sold
```

"Remember that 'Work in Process' and 'Finished Goods' include the materials, labor, and factory-overhead costs used to make them," Holmes added. "So, although we add these costs at the beginning, we subtract them for any unfinished or unsold item at the end of the period. To, perhaps, oversimplify this, if we began with a million dollars in inventory, added half a million dollars in materials, labor, and overhead, but didn't sell anything, we would end up with an extra half a million in inventory but no Cost of Goods Sold. The Balance Sheet would show the larger Inventory and a reduction in some other asset, like Cash."

"I'm afraid to ask this," Sue confessed, "but aren't there different ways of figuring the value of the inventory?"

Holmes sighed. "Yes, there are. Perhaps the most obvious way is to figure that you sell the items in the same order as you place them in inventory. This is called First In, First Out, or FIFO. Another way to determine inventory costs is to figure the cost of any item you sell as being the cost of replacing it, which is the same as the cost of the last item you put into inventory. This is called Last In, First Out. You can also average the costs of items purchased during the year. There are numerous tax and accuracy ramifications for each method, which we needn't go into here. Depending upon which method is used, the accountants calculate the costs in somewhat different ways. All we need to understand here is the kinds of expenses that are included in the Cost of Goods Sold."

"Wouldn't 'Last In, First Out' leave us with a lot of old goods in inventory?" Sue asked.

"No, we don't put cost tags on individual items in inventory," Holmes explained. "All of the individual items of the same product are considered completely interchangeable so far as bookkeeping goes. Even though the warehouse will generally move out the oldest items first, the accountants are free to assign the costs in any way: FIFO, LIFO, or some averaging method.

"Regardless of the method used, the accountants normally adjust the entry for the Inventory to reflect the lower of its original cost and its current market value or at the lower of cost or market. Therefore, if the price of our product and raw materials drops significantly during the period, the reduction in value would increase the Cost of Goods Sold. However, if the price increases, the value will remain at the original cost (reflecting the lower of the two values)."

Operating Expenses

"I think a number of items in this next section are pretty self-evident," Greg commented, "like the payroll, office supplies, and the office's share of building maintenance, insurance, and depreciation. However, there are some items that I would expect to fall under the Cost of Goods Sold, like Research and Development, Warranty payments, and Scrap."

EXPENSES	
Salary Payroll	13,614
Hourly Payroll	5,179
Payroll Taxes	2,819
Benefits	1,924
Research & Development	1,776
Warranty	1,317
Depreciation	829
Scrap	4,380
Supplies (Office & Operating)	252
Repair & Maintenance	1,243
Advertising & Marketing	89
Telephone	740
Utilities	1,273
Insurance	2,649
Taxes (Real Estate, etc.)	577
Bad Debts	2,323
Other	422
TOTAL	**41,406**

"In a way," Holmes conceded. "However, we want to segregate the actual cost of making the lamps from the other factors. As Sue pointed out earlier, this enables us to directly compare our manufacturing costs with those of potential suppliers and rival companies. And even if we did buy products from other suppliers, we might still do research and development for the designs and would certainly have warranty and scrap costs. I might add that not all scrap is caused by quality problems; it is often due to ordering more items than can be sold or having some items go out of style. And warranty costs can be affected by sales decisions to shorten or lengthen the warranty period, change what is covered by the warranty, and so on—decisions that affect costs independently from what the factory does."

"Still," Greg persisted, "I would think that a poor factory might seem to produce lamps cheaply, but the added costs of warranty work, returns, and scrap could make the ultimate cost higher than that of a higher-quality factory with a somewhat higher initial cost."

"That's certainly possible," Holmes agreed. "But listing these costs separately makes them stand out, especially when we look at the five-year figures."

"Okay," Sue said. "What puzzles me is the 'Payroll Taxes' item. Don't the workers pay their own taxes?"

"Of course," Holmes agreed. "But they pay the taxes out of the money we pay them. Remember the 'Other Accrued Expenses' item on the Balance Sheet? That includes money set aside for the future payment of taxes withheld from workers' paychecks. So we distinguish here between the money paid directly to the employees through payroll checks, which the company must pay when due (Accrued Expenses on the Balance Sheet), and the company's portion of taxes such as Social Security (FICA), which are expenses the company pays out of its pocket (payroll taxes). In addition, the company has benefits as an expense. These include the company's portion of such items as health and dental insurance."

"So Accrued Expenses are another way of tracking money that the company can use temporarily before paying it out?" Greg asked.

"Yes, but I don't think you want to get into the intricacies of how this shows up elsewhere," Holmes answered.

Taxes

"Mr. Holmes, you talked about deducting income taxes to arrive at the company's Net Profit or the net Retained Earnings," Sue observed. "However, the 'Income Taxes' line here is blank."

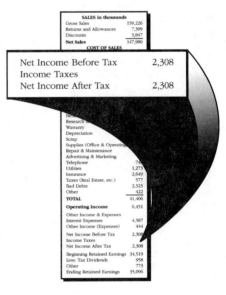

"That's because you and Greg are paying the taxes as individuals," Holmes answered. "FerMon is an 'S Corporation,' which means that it is treated as a partnership, not a corporation, for tax purposes. Therefore, you pay the income tax on your personal tax returns according to your ownership share in the company. Companies with 'C Corporation' status pay the federal income taxes directly, and, accordingly, those payments would be listed on this line."

"I guess I let my tax preparer worry about those details," Greg confessed. "But why don't we let the company pay the taxes?"

"Ideally, because this way can save on taxes," Holmes replied. "When the corporation pays taxes before paying you dividends, you have to pay taxes twice, once as income taxes by the company and again as personal taxes on the dividends you receive from the company."

"Well, then, why don't all companies use the 'S Corporation' method?" Greg countered.

"First of all, the 'S' structure can only be used by companies with relatively few stockholders," Holmes answered. "Secondly, as with most choices in life, the 'S' method holds potential drawbacks as well. You are responsible for paying taxes on all the company's profits even if you receive only a small dividend payment or no dividends at all."

The cousins' eyes widened as they contemplated this. Then Sue burst out, "I've been wondering why we continued receiving some dividends even when the company was heavily borrowing money for its expansion. Do you suppose that the management wanted to avoid upsetting us by leaving us with a big tax bill but no income to pay it?"

"Actually," Holmes pointed out, "the company has been giving you the money for the taxes, which is listed near the bottom as the 'Tax Dividends.' The 'Other' item is largely, if not exclusively, the dividend you get to pocket."

"In any case," Sue continued, "now we really need get to the bottom of the company's financial situation."

"Yeah," Greg agreed. "We certainly don't want to be left holding the bag!"

"Okay," Holmes agreed. "Now that we've looked at the individual entries, let's see what we can find out from the five-year statements."

Types of Business Structures

You may operate your business or organization under any one of several organizational structures. Each type of structure has certain advantages and disadvantages that should be considered.

A **Sole Proprietorship** is one individual or married couple in business alone. Sole proprietorships are the most common form of business structure. This type of business is simple to form and operate, and may enjoy greater flexibility of management and fewer legal controls. However, the business owner is personally liable for all debts incurred by the business.

A **General Partnership** is composed of two or more persons (usually not a married couple) who agree to contribute money, labor, an/or skill to a business. Each partner shares the profits, losses, and management of the business, and each partner is personally and equally liable for debts of the partnership. Formal terms of the partnership are usually contained in a written partnership agreement.

A **Limited Partnership** is composed of one or more general partners and one or more limited partners. The general partners manage the business and share full in its profits and losses. Limited partners share in the profits of the business, but their losses are limited to the extent of their investment. Limited partners are usually not involved in the day-to-day operations of the business.

A **Limited Liability Partnership** is similar to a General Partnership except that normally a partner does not have personal liability for the negligence of another partner. This business structure is used most commonly by professionals such as accountants and lawyers.

A **Corporation C Corp** or **Subchapter (S)** is a more complex business structure. As a chartered legal entity, a corporation has certain rights, privileges, and liabilities beyond those of an individual. Doing business as a corporation may yield tax or financial benefits, but these can be offset by other considerations, such as increased licensing fees or decreased personal control. Corporations may be formed for profit or nonprofit purposes.

The **Limited Liability Company (LLC)** and the **Limited Liability Partnership (LLP)** are relatively new business structures. An LLC or LLP is formed by one or more individuals or entities through a special written agreement. The agreement details the organization of the LLC or LLP, including: provisions for management, assign ability of interests, and distribution of profits or losses. Limited liability companies and limited liability partnerships are permitted to engage in any lawful, for profit business or activity other than banking or insurance.

CHAPTER 8

The Statement: Five-Year Comparisons

The "Bottom Line"

Holmes spread out the five-year Income Statement on the table.

"I know you have argued against focusing too much on the bottom line," Greg said, "but I can't help noticing that the Net Income has fallen to about a fifth of what it was in the first year."

"That's true," Sue agreed. "And it has fallen even more dramatically from what it was in the third year, which is only two years ago. Aren't these pretty clear signs of trouble?"

"They certainly demand further investigation," Holmes conceded, "especially when there is an apparent trend. However, there can be perfectly good reasons for profits to diminish for a few years, such as investments related to updating or expanding operations. There can also be one-time deductions, like writing off a unique loss or meeting new regulatory requirements. Such temporary drops in profits do not usually presage disaster; indeed, good investments greatly enhance the company's long-term prospects."

"So you're saying we shouldn't pay much attention to profits?" Greg demanded.

"Not at all," Holmes replied. "Profits pay for expenses, dividends, and growth. I'm just saying that we cannot stop with the 'bottom line' but must look at other parts of the financial statement to find out how the company is running. Look at it this way: if we were scrutinizing the financial statement of two years ago, which ended with what is now Year Three, we would see profits increasing by a considerable amount over a two-year period. According to the 'bottom line,' everything was looking up."

"That's true," Greg conceded. "I suppose something big could have happened in Year Four to change things."

"That's possible, but it's more likely that the trouble is connected with the expansions or longer-standing conditions that the expansions failed to correct," Holmes said. "Assuming that these reports are honest and thorough, the figures for Year Three should also show harbingers of the

Income Statement

(in thousands)

	Year 1	Year 2	Year 3	Year 4	Year 5
Gross Sales	132,262	151,923	171,509	165,114	159,226
Returns and Allowances	2,568	5,079	4,919	6,542	7,399
Discounts	1,284	1,741	2,623	2,804	3,847
Net Sales	128,410	145,103	163,967	155,768	147,980
COST OF SALES					
Material	44,687	50,728	56,864	55,905	53,569
Labor	21,316	24,522	28,202	28,848	27,524
Depreciation	1,746	1,669	1,804	1,838	1,820
Other Manufacturing Overhead	16,231	16,527	16,757	17,835	17,210
Total Cost of Sales	83,980	93,446	103,627	104,426	100,123
Gross Profit	44,430	51,657	60,340	51,342	47,857
OPERATING EXPENSES					
Salary Payroll	11,043	14,975	14,921	14,954	13,614
Hourly Payroll	4,494	5,079	5,739	5,452	5,179
Payroll Taxes	2,331	3,008	3,099	3,061	2,819
Benefits	1,669	1,741	1,804	1,713	1,924
Research & Development	3,981	1,973	2,771	1,760	1,776
Warranty	321	334	869	1,184	1,317
Depreciation	539	760	880	771	829
Scrap	886	987	2,607	4,439	4,380
Supplies (Office & Operating)	257	218	164	234	252
Repair & Maintenance	360	276	344	1,168	1,243
Advertising & Marketing	578	566	312	234	89
Telephone	449	479	672	701	740
Utilities	732	813	1,148	1,153	1,273
Insurance	1,143	1,132	1,427	1,916	2,649
Taxes (Real Estate, etc.)	398	421	508	545	577
Bad Debts	334	377	1,115	1,807	2,323
Other	2,459	1,338	1,153	967	422
TOTAL	31,974	34,477	39,533	42,059	41,406
Operating Income	12,456	17,180	20,807	9,283	6,451
Other Income & Expenses					
Interest Expenses	2,311	2,902	4,099	4,206	4,587
Other Income (Expenses)	257	290	328	234	444
Net Income Before Tax	10,402	14,568	17,036	5,311	2,308
Income Taxes					
Net Income After Tax	10,402	14,568	17,036	5,311	2,308
Beginning Retained Earnings	21,569	25,290	28,932	33,191	34,519
Less: Tax Dividends	4,317	6,046	7,070	2,204	958
Other	2,364	4,880	5,707	1,779	773
Ending Retained Earnings	25,290	28,932	33,191	34,519	35,096

downward trends that began the very next year."

"Well, what about the disturbing items we found on the Balance Sheet, like the increases in Accounts Receivable, Inventory, and short-term credit?" Sue asked.

"Those are examples of the further digging I'm recommending," Holmes agreed. "But, to avoid confusion, let's postpone looking at the third-year status and trends until we have gone through the entire financial statement. And, right now, let's focus on the Income Statement. Net Sales is a good place to begin, because that is the major source of our income."

Sales

"Overall," Greg observed, "the Net Sales seem to have the same pattern as the Net Income: rising through the third year, and then falling during the past two years. However, the Net Sales do not seem to have fallen as dramatically as the Net Income."

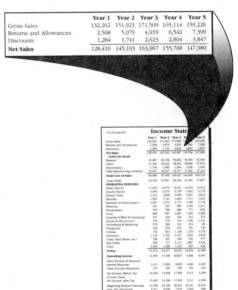

	Year 1	Year 2	Year 3	Year 4	Year 5
Gross Sales	132,262	151,923	171,509	165,114	159,226
Returns and Allowances	2,568	5,079	4,919	6,542	7,399
Discounts	1,284	1,741	2,623	2,804	3,847
Net Sales	128,410	145,103	163,967	155,768	147,980

"That's a good observation," Holmes said, "but let's focus on Sales for now. How would you compare the trends in Gross and Net Sales?"

"Gross Sales don't seem to have fallen as dramatically," Sue replied. "Between Years Three and Five, Gross Sales fell by about $12 million, but the Net Sales fell by about $16 million."

"Yeah, and the reason's pretty obvious," Greg joined in. "The Returns and the Discounts amounts went up by about $4 million during the past two years. In fact, just by eyeballing it, I'd say that each of those amounts has about tripled since Year One."

"That's terrible!" Sue exclaimed. "It looks like we have some real quality problems and that they're getting worse."

"Yeah, and the jumps in discounts suggest that we're finding it harder and harder to get people to buy our lamps," Greg added.

"Those are logical inferences," Holmes commended them. "We will have to find out where the returns problem lies: in the quality of the lamps, the filling and shipping of orders, or in the quality of our customers."

"How would the customers affect our quality?" Sue asked.

"Poorer-quality customers may cause some of the damage themselves through poor handling, or they may order larger quantities than they can sell, through poor planning or as a way of earning discounts, and then return what they can't sell as 'unsatisfactory.' That, of course, is speculation; we should look into our own quality issues first."

Cost of Sales

"Well, if Net Sales went down by $16 million during the last two years, how come the Cost of Sales went down by only $3.5 million?" Greg asked.

COST OF SALES					
Material	44,687	50,728	56,864	55,905	53,569
Labor	21,316	24,522	28,202	28,848	27,524
Depreciation	1,746	1,669	1,804	1,838	1,820
Other Manufacturing Overhead	16,231	16,527	16,757	17,835	17,210
Total Cost of Sales	83,980	93,446	103,627	104,426	100,123

"That's an excellent question," Holmes said. "Since we count only the costs of the lamps we sell, not those that remain in Inventory, one would expect the Cost of Goods Sold to go up and down rather evenly with sales. An obvious inference is that we are making less on what we sell."

"Are you talking about the Gross Margin?" Sue asked.

"Yes: dividing the Cost of Sales by the Net Sales tells us what percentage of our selling price is needed to pay for the production of the lamps," Holmes agreed. "Subtracting that percentage from one hundred percent gives us our Gross Margin."

$$\frac{\text{Cost of Sales}}{\text{Net Sales}} = \text{Cost percentage}$$

100% − Cost percentage = Gross Margin

"We can also calculate the Gross Margin by dividing Gross Profit by Net Sales. Using either calculation, we find that our Gross Margin has fallen from 34.6% in the first year to 32.3% in the fifth year. To put this way, the cost of making the lamps has increased from 65.4% to 67.7% or we could be selling lamps for lower prices with costs not being reduced accordingly."

"Well, a drop of 2.3 cents doesn't sound so terrible," Sue remarked.

"Not when you're talking about change for a dollar," Holmes said, "but 2.3 percent of the Gross Sales is almost $3.7 million, which is about 1.6 times the Net Income for last year."

"But it looks like things had gone better during the second and third years," Greg observed.

"Let's check that," Holmes said, returning to his calculator. "Yes, in the third year, the Gross Margin had improved to 36.8%, so that means that it has slipped by 4.5% during the past two years."

"So we have definite grounds for arguing that there are troubles which we need to investigate further," Sue concluded.

Quality Problems

After studying the statement for a few moments, Holmes continued. "I think Greg has already pinpointed a major factor: Returns and Discounts. Over the past five years, Gross Sales increased by about $27 million, but Net Sales increased by only $19.6 million. The major difference lies in the $4.8 million increase in Returns and Allowances and the $2.6 million in Discounts.

"Since we have already spent time speculating about quality problems, based on the increases in Returns and Allowances and in Discounts, we might as well look at the related entries in the 'Operating Expenses' section."

"Well, I see that the 'Warranty' expense has more than quadrupled," Greg noted. "This could indicate increasing returns of poorer-quality lamps."

"Or," Sue added, "the offering of more generous warranties as a sales incentive."

"I suppose so," Greg said. "However, even if we are offering longer warranties as a sales incentive, the large increases in this expense must be paying for more than printing new certificates—the increases must be covering actual returns."

"And additional Returns and Allowances could tie in with what I heard about the making of cheaper lamps," Sue added.

"This, again, is a question that goes beyond the detail provided in financial statements," Holmes noted. "What we are finding is that the statements are pointing us in the direction for further research. Notice that the 'Scrap' entry has also risen sharply; it is almost five times what it was in Year One. Earlier, I said that scrap could be caused by overproduction, outdated items, and other non-quality matters. However, as we see the combination of related entries, the existence of quality problems seems increasingly probable.

"I would also like to call your attention to the 'Research and Development' entries: we are spending less than half of what we did four years ago."

"How does that fit into the quality issue?" Greg asked.

"It could mean that we're not putting enough effort into improving our quality," Holmes said. "It could also mean that, by failing to develop new products, we are gradually falling behind our competitors. That could partly explain the growing inventory, increased returns, sagging customer interest, and reduced profit margins. Businesses that greatly reduce their research and development often show improved profits for a couple of years, after which profits begin to plummet."

"Why the delay?" Sue asked.

"Because it takes time to get new products into production and on the market," Holmes explained. "In the interim, we have eliminated an expense and are gleaning the profit from the earlier product development. After that, competitors' newer products begin to outpace our aging ones."

"Now that you mention it," Greg added, "the drop in Research and Development from Year One to Year Three is about $2.2 million, which is almost exactly the amount of our Net Income, or profit. So you could say that we really didn't make any money this past year but simply took the money out of Research and Development."

"In a way," Holmes said, "though, of course, the way we arrived at our present situation is much more complex than a simple transfer of funds from one account to another."

Operating Expenses

"Before looking at any more details of the Operating Expenses, let's step back and look at how they have varied with our Net Sales," Holmes advised.

"I'd say they've gone up by about $10 million," Greg observed.

OPERATING EXPENSES					
Salary Payroll	11,043	14,975	14,921	14,954	13,614
Hourly Payroll	4,494	5,079	5,739	5,452	5,179
Payroll Taxes	2,331	3,008	3,099	3,061	2,819
Benefits	1,669	1,741	1,804	1,713	1,924
Research & Development	3,981	1,973	2,771	1,760	1,776
Warranty	321	334	869	1,184	1,317
Depreciation	539	760	880	771	829
Scrap	886	987	2,607	4,439	4,380
Supplies (Office & Operating)	257	218	164	234	252
Repair & Maintenance	360	276	344	1,168	1,243
Advertising & Marketing	578	566	312	234	89
Telephone	449	479	672	701	740
Utilities	732	813	1,148	1,153	1,273
Insurance	1,143	1,132	1,427	1,916	2,649
Taxes (Real Estate, etc.)	398	421	508	545	577
Bad Debts	334	377	1,115	1,807	2,323
Other	2,459	1,338	1,153	967	422
TOTAL	31,974	34,477	39,533	42,059	41,406

"They did go down about half a million during this past year," Sue added, "but not nearly as much as our sales and profits did."

"Quite so," Holmes said. "As Greg remarked earlier, we would expect the Cost of Goods Sold to vary directly with sales. What about Operating Expenses?"

The cousins scanned the items under this listing, and then Sue said, "Well, it would seem that a lot of them, like the people working in the administration, the building, and their expenses and supplies would cost the same whether or not sales were down."

"Exactly," Holmes agreed. "They fall under the category of 'fixed expenses.' These expenses, of course, are not absolutely unvarying; they tend to increase as people receive raises, taxes rise, aging buildings and equipment need increased maintenance or replacement, and so on. They are 'fixed' only in the sense that they remain largely the same whether production and sales are up or down."

"Actually," Sue observed, "it looks like the Salary and Hourly Payrolls went down this past year."

"That could mean the company has tried to improve profits by cutting some fixed expenses," Holmes noted. "Expenses that vary closely with changes in sales volume are called 'variable expenses.' Deducting these variable expenses from sales gives us the 'contribution margin,' or profits that are available to pay for our 'fixed' expenses. If the contribution margin just equals the amount of our fixed expenses, we would have zero profit before tax, or be at our 'Break-Even Point.'

He wrote the following on the flip chart:

Net Sales – Variable Expenses = Contribution Margin

Contribution Margin – Fixed Expenses = Net Profit before Tax

"When the Net Profit before Tax is zero, we can say that the sales figure that got us to zero profit is our Break-Even Point for sales." Holmes added the following to the flip chart:

	Net Sales
–	Cost of Sales
–	Operating Expenses
	Contribution Margin
	Contribution Margin
–	Other Expenses
	Break-even Point

"If our Contribution Margin is not enough to pay for our fixed expenses, then we either have to accept losses or begin to cut the fixed expenses," Holmes concluded.

"Like the 'three-martini lunch?'" Greg asked.

"Certainly any discretionary spending," Holmes said. "And one can reduce spending on consultants and temporary help in many cases. In the longer term, one might find a less expensive office building. Unfortunately, temporary and permanent layoffs are a frequent means of cutting fixed expenses—easier to do, and easier to end when income improves."

"Well, if the payroll has been cut, how come the 'Benefits' went up?" Sue asked.

"Benefits, especially health insurance, tend to keep rising, and events beyond the company's control, like statewide or nationwide layoffs, can push up the cost of unemployment insurance. However, the Benefits item increased by the relatively small sum of $255 thousand during the past five years. This is worth noting but is probably not our major concern, since we are trying to account for a $15 million drop in net income during the past two years."

"If you're looking at the big increases we haven't covered yet," Greg volunteered, "I see that 'Repairs and Maintenance' has more than tripled, 'Insurance' has more than doubled, and 'Bad Debts' has gone up more than seven times since Year One."

"The Bad Debts would seem related to the increases in Accounts Receivable," Sue speculated. "We're getting poorer-quality customers, offering bigger discounts, and suffering from deadbeats among them."

"That's possibly true," Holmes replied. "However, the 'Bad Debts' item represents more than actual write-offs. Remember the conservative way in accrual accounting. As soon as an order is shipped, we enter what is owed in Accounts Receivable. However, experience shows that a certain percentage of debts will never be collected. To keep our income estimates reasonably accurate, the accountants reduce the Accounts Receivable by this 'Bad Debts' entry, which is an estimate of future write-offs from the receivables."

"I guess that makes sense," Sue conceded. "It would be confusing to operate a business assuming there were a certain amount of assets and then suddenly having to subtract bad debts as they occurred."

"Well, I can see that," Greg admitted. "But I'm still troubled by the fact that the 'Bad Debts' entry has grown from a third of a million to $2.3 million, or about seven times, while the Accounts Receivable has grown from $17 million to $26 million, or only about fifty percent."

"That's a good point," Holmes agreed. "Of course, the accountants do have to keep track of actual losses and adjust the 'Bad Debts' estimate up or down accordingly. So, although the Year Five entry may not represent the actual write-off for the year, it probably reflects a growing problem."

"What about the growing costs of 'Repair and Maintenance' and 'Insurance'? Why should they go up when we bought a new plant?" Sue asked.

"Presumably, the 'Repair and Maintenance' item applies only to the administration buildings and equipment," Holmes pointed out. "However, the 'Insurance' entry may apply to all our property. We would have to find this out from the management. In either case, property and liability insurance premiums sometimes increase sharply in response to major outside events, like natural disasters and terrorist attacks. If we come across other indicators, we would then look into the possibilities of aging buildings and equipment or an extensive remodeling and updating project."

"There's one item that has gone down to almost nothing: 'Advertising and Marketing,' something I would have expected the company to spend more on, given the problem with sales," Greg commented.

"Yes, and the downward trend seems to have coincided with the investment in the new plant," Sue added. "Does that indicate that the company decided to rely upon lower prices to increase sales?"

"Or perhaps, perceiving no immediate return on this money, the management saw it as an easy place to make cuts," Holmes remarked. "Companies often make short-sighted cuts when continued or even increased spending might produce better results. Since the cuts began in the second year, when profits were rising, this might have been a deliberate strategy, such as relying mainly upon price cuts to increase sales. We will have to ask the management about this as well."

Operating Income

"So, after deducting the Operating Expenses from the Gross Profit, we are left with about $6.5 million," Holmes continued. "This remainder is called the 'Operating Income' because it represents what the company has earned after deducting all the expenses of its normal operations, both the factory and the office."

"So, basically, this is the money available for paying off non-operating expenses like interest and taxes?" Greg asked.

"That's right. To a certain extent, you might consider it a measure of the company's present strength as a manufacturing business."

"In that case," Sue remarked, "it looks like we're getting weaker fast: the Operating Income for Year Five is only about half of what it was in Year One, and less than a third of what it was in Year Three."

Other Income and Expenses

"There are only two items here," Holmes noted, "but they account for cutting this year's Net Income, or profits, in half. Actually, 'Other Income' adds $444 thousand to the profits, so all the reduction comes from the 'Interest Expense.' Does this remind you of any other figures that we have covered?"

"The Balance Sheet," Greg responded. "As I recall, we were concerned about the sharp increases in short-term loans and Accounts Payable."

"Yes, and curious about the shrinking long-term loans," Sue added.

"Excellent," Holmes commended them. "You're remembering the big issues and making connections. You'll be experts in no time!"

"Interest payments seem to be a growing problem," Greg noted. "They have almost doubled compared with Year One."

"And they have grown steadily since the big jump in Year Two," Sue added. "In fact, if they grow much more, they could eat up all of the profits."

"Yes, the combination of falling sales, shrinking margins, and growing debts does appear to form a picture of a company in financial trouble," Holmes agreed. "The data suggesting poorer-quality products and customers also raise questions about the company's ability to increase the Operating Income we need to pay off the debts and finance the necessary improvements for increasing profits, such as reinvigorating research and development, doing more marketing and advertising, and upgrading our plants and equipment."

"It's curious that, with our main income going down, the 'Other Income' has increased," Greg observed.

"I suspect that is related to the sale of equipment that is no longer used, but we need to ask management for specific information about the increase."

Areas for Investigation

"One thing I want to find out for sure is whether our quality has slipped," Greg declared. "Our parents and grandparents built FerMon on a reputation for high quality, and I fear that losing that reputation could mean disaster."

"That could be severely damaging," Holmes agreed. "And, once lost, a reputation can be very difficult to regain. So we need to find out why sales are down: are we selling less expensive items (different mix of products), simply selling less (reduced demand for our products), selling at lower prices (or proving unable to raise prices to meet our increased costs), or a combination of these factors?"

"What about the years when sales went up?" Sue asked.

"Yes, we need to know what happened then, too," Holmes agreed. "Were we getting a bigger share of our market at the expense of our competitors or sharing a broader upsurge in business? If we expanded more than the average for our industry, was it because we introduced new products or entered a new market?"

"Will the financial report tell us these things?" Greg asked.

"Sometimes there may be references to them in the introductory messages or in special notes," Holmes answered. "For the most part, though, we will have to obtain information about the industry and competitors from specialized sources, and information about our company from the management. Knowing what we are looking for will make the job easier and help us select and interpret the data we are examining."

"Are we going to do that now?" Sue asked.

"No, we have to finish with the financial statements first," Holmes said. "The Cash Flow Statement should give us the clearest picture of how we are doing in the all important area of cash management. If, as we suspect, there is a growing problem with shrinking profits and expanding debts, we should obtain a dramatic picture of this through the Cash Flow Statement."

CHAPTER 9

The Cash Flow Statement

The Major Cause of Business Failure

Holmes spread out the Income statement for the previous year.

After the cousins had studied it for a few minutes, Greg said, "This seems to list the same items as the other statements—'Net Income,' 'Accounts Payable,' 'Inventories.' Only the labels of the totals for each section, like 'Net Cash Provided,' seem different."

"And the figures," Sue added.

"That's true," Holmes agreed. "This entire **Cash Flow Statement is derived from the Balance Sheet and the Income Statement.** Like the Income Statement, the Cash Flow Statement reflects account activity over a period of time. As we saw, the Balance Sheet shows us how much the company's assets are growing or shrinking and how those assets are financed. The Income statement shows us how profitably the assets are being managed. These additional calculations provide us with another crucial view of the company—how it manages its cash."

"Why is that crucial?" Greg asked. "Cash seems to make up

Statement of Cash Flows	
(in thousands)	
Cash Flows from Operations:	
Net Income	2,308
Depreciation	2,651
Changes in:	
Accounts Receivable	(168)
Inventories	(664)
Prepaid Expenses	(229)
Other Assets	(637)
Accounts Payable	677
Accrued Expenses	(41)
Deferred Taxes	92
Net Cash Provided	3,989
Cash Flows from Investing:	
Purchase of Fixed Assets	(1,957)
Net Cash Used	(1,957)
Cash Flows from Financing:	
Change in Notes Payable	362
Change in Long Term Debt	(772)
Change in Common Stock	0
Payment of Dividends	(1,731)
Net Cash from Investing	(2,141)
Net Cash Flow	(109)
Cash at Beginning of Year	6,092
Cash at End of Year	5,983

less than ten percent of the total assets on the Balance Sheet. And I thought you said that the most important managerial decisions about profits concern reinvesting them in the company, because that's where most future profits will be made."

"That's also true," Holmes conceded. "However, you could say that the primary reason for most business failures is poor cash management. They couldn't pay their bills on time."

"Is that just another way of saying 'losing money'?" Sue demanded.

"It could be, but many companies whose Balance Sheets and Income Statements showed profits ended up in bankruptcy because of cash shortages. If you can't pay your employees, rent, utilities, and suppliers on time, you'll have a hard time keeping your doors open."

Keeping the Doors Open

"Let's start with a simple example: suppose a company consistently allows its customers between sixty and ninety days to pay what they owe but pays its creditors immediately or within thirty days. On the Balance Sheet, the Accounts Receivable would make the assets appear substantial, while the low amount in Accounts Payable would make its liabilities appear relatively small. However, the cash could eventually shrink to less than what is needed to cover the company's regular bills. Ironically, cash-flow problems can especially affect rapidly expanding companies, whose cash becomes tied up in promising new ventures and paying off expansion loans."

"So temporary cash shortages can ruin a company even if, in the course of the year, the profits will more than cover the expenses?" Greg asked.

"Yes," Holmes insisted. "Ideally, if expenses and income were evenly spaced throughout the year and the assets are being managed properly, a profitable company would have no problem with cash flow. But a reservoir can go dry with a big summer demand even though the coming winter snows and spring rains will bring more than enough water to cover the past year's demand."

The cousins pondered this for a moment. Then Sue said, "In that case, we would have to get our customers to pay sooner and get our creditors to grant us extensions."

"And if we couldn't do that, we'd have to take out short-term loans," Greg added.

"Loans would add interest expenses and increase the amount that had to be repaid during the coming months," Holmes pointed out. "Eventually, a company with cash-flow problems could be forced to sell a profitable asset, perhaps an investment or even a plant, to meet these short-term obligations. Such an emergency sale could lose money and hurt the company in the long run."

"So that is what is known as a liquidity problem," Sue concluded.

"Exactly," Holmes agreed. "To keep healthy, a company needs a 'positive' cash flow, which simply means that more cash is coming in than is going out. Obviously, a 'negative' cash flow is the reverse: more cash going out than is coming in."

Greg scratched his head. "So you're saying that paper profits do not pay for anything. Does that mean having to keep large amounts of cash in the drawer?"

"Not at all, but you must be able to put your hands on cash when you have to pay your expenses. The cash could be in bank accounts on which you can freely draw, short-term investments, or financial instruments like high-quality bonds that you can easily sell for cash—in short, you need what financial experts call 'liquid assets.'"

> *To keep healthy, a company needs a 'positive' cash flow, which simply means that more cash is coming in than is going out.*

"Negative" Entries

"Most of the entries are in parentheses and are printed in red," Sue observed. "I thought that indicated losses."

"That's true on the Balance Sheet and the Income Statement," Holmes explained, "but not on the Cash Flow Statement. What this statement shows is how various items have increased or decreased our cash."

"So the parentheses indicate a reduction in cash?" Greg asked.

"That's right."

"Well, isn't that like a loss?" Sue asked.

"Not necessarily," Holmes answered. "Look at Accounts Receivable and Inventory: the negative numbers mean that cash has gone into them. However, they should eventually be exchanged for cash, so one cannot call these amounts losses."

"But didn't you say that tying up too much money in Accounts Receivable and Inventory could cause trouble?" Greg persisted.

"Yes. Disproportionate increases in these accounts—increases far in excess of the rate of growth in sales—could indicate problems, such as customers who are poor credit risks and inventory items that are not selling. However, we can detect such increases in the Balance Sheet. Our focus here is strictly on how much cash we generate for paying our bills. If there is a cash-flow problem, the negative figures will show us where the cash is draining off."

"Can we at least regard negative figures as, well, negative results?" Sue asked.

"Not really," Holmes replied. "For example, a reduction in Accounts Payable or Notes Payable causes a reduction in cash, but paying off bills and owing less isn't all bad. On the other side, an increase in Accounts Receivable would appear as a reduction in cash, even if this were in step with increased Sales."

"Wait a minute," Greg objected. "How does billing a customer cost us cash?"

Holmes signaled "stop" with his right hand. "Okay, it's time to look more closely at what these calculations mean."

Checking Your Wallet

"Suppose you wandered into a gift shop while you were on vacation and wanted to buy an item without charging it, because you wanted to remain within the spending limits you had set for yourself. What would you do?"

"I'd check to see how much money I had in my wallet," Greg responded. "And then I'd calculate how much of it I needed for the rest of the trip."

"I'd also try to remember how much cash I had elsewhere, like the hotel safe," Sue added.

"How about checking your home equity, bank accounts, or investments?" Holmes asked.

"Not if I were trying to limit my spending to my cash on hand," Greg answered. "I take it that you are setting this up as a cash-flow example."

"Yes, I am," Holmes admitted. "And if you consistently found yourself short of cash on your trip, would you question your income or investments?"

"No, I'd have to decide whether my original calculations about how much money to take on the trip were too conservative or whether I was imprudently departing from a good plan by wanting to spend too much," Sue said.

"That's a good way of putting it," Holmes commended her. "In the same way, checking the Cash Flow Statement does not necessarily involve redoing all the calculations about the value of the company or the profitability of its operations and investments. We are narrowing our focus to how much money we have available for our planned expenses. Of course, if we uncover a negative cash flow, we will have to dig deeper and, as Sue said, figure out whether we are carelessly exceeding our budget or have allocated too little cash for our needs. We may also uncover deeper problems, such as excessive interest charges for short-term loans, that will cause us to re-evaluate the information on the Balance Sheet and Income Statement. But we should begin with the simple question of how much cash there is."

"So far we've been talking about cash shortages," Greg pointed out. "Can there also be a problem of excessive cash?"

"Of course," Holmes replied. "As you mentioned a little earlier, reinvesting in the company is a major priority. If the Cash Flow Statement shows a lot more money on hand than is needed to meet regular expenses, then we'd have to look further into that, too."

Increasing Assets and Paying Bills as Reducing Cash

The cousins pondered the Cash Flow Statement for a moment. Then Sue said, "Okay, I see where putting more money into Inventory could be construed as a reduction in cash. And the same would hold true for Other Assets."

"I guess I can see this for Accounts Payable, too," Greg added. "As we pay off bills and this entry decreases, we have less cash."

"What about Prepaid Expenses?" asked Holmes.

"Well, if we paid more for things like insurance, that would also take up cash," Sue replied.

Greg scratched his head, then brightened. "I was confused about this because we list 'Prepaid Expenses' as an asset that is gradually used up. But now I see that, although we have the value of, say, ongoing insurance coverage, we have actually paid out all the cash for it."

The Effect of Accrued Expenses on Cash

"And what about Accrued Expenses?"

Sue frowned in thought. "If I remember right, those are other amounts that we owe, like the payroll and employee benefits. If the amounts we owe decrease, that means we paid out extra cash. That much is easy to understand. And I suppose that, when we owe more, it means, in a way, that we temporarily have extra cash, though I don't see how simply owing more gives us more cash."

"To speak technically, the Income Statement is based upon accrued expenses," Holmes explained. "This means that, in the Income Statement, we have already subtracted the amounts we owe from the Net Income figure. However, because this year's additional amounts in Accounts Payable and Accrued Expenses have not yet been paid, we still have that cash on hand. Again, we are not figuring profits here, but ready cash."

After a few moments of silence, Greg said, "So, less technically, for the sake of making the Cash Flow calculations, we are acting as if all profits start as cash. Then we calculate how the changes in each category during the past year would add to or take away from that amount."

"That's it," Holmes agreed. "For example, since Accounts Receivable grew by $168,000 last year, that amount represents, at the time of the statement, less cash on hand due to our higher investment in receivables."

"But isn't that treating Accounts Receivable as a loss?" Sue asked.

"Not at all. Let's say, for simplicity's sake, that Accounts Receivable grew by the same amount as our profit: how much new cash would we have gained from these profits?"

"None," Greg admitted. "The amount added by the Net Income would be canceled by the amount subtracted by the Accounts Receivable."

"But our Income statement would still show a profit?"

"Yes," Sue said. "However, we'd probably be in trouble without some increase in cash."

"And there you have the difference between the Income statement and the Cash Flow Statement, and why we also need the latter," Holmes said.

"But what about the Accrued Expenses?" Greg asked. "How does spending less on payroll and professional fees cost us cash?"

"Ultimately, it doesn't," Holmes admitted. "Remember, though, we aren't figuring profits here, just cash on hand. Although the Income statement shows Accrued Expenses as subtractions from profit, while we are holding the money to be paid later, it is still cash on hand. In the current statements, because we are holding less money for these expenses at the end of this year than we did at the end of the previous year, we actually have less cash on hand from this source."

"But having extra money earmarked for payment to others doesn't mean we have more money to spend," Sue objected.

"That's true," Holmes conceded. "However, our Net Profit and Retained Earnings entries give us a better idea of how much we have to budget for new assets and dividends. Here, we are simply looking at our liquidity."

The Effect of Changes on Cash

"Let's sum up the ways in which changes in the items from the Income and Balance statements affect cash," Holmes suggested. He drew the following table on the flip chart:

Item	Adds Cash by
Accounts Receivable	Decreasing
Inventories	Decreasing
Prepaid Expenses	Decreasing
Other Assets	Decreasing
Accounts Payable	Increasing
Accrued Expenses	Increasing
Deferred Taxes	Increasing
Fixed Assets	Decreasing
Notes Payable	Increasing
Long-Term Debt	Increasing
Common Stock	Increasing
Dividends Payable	Decreasing

Greg scratched his head. "According to this table, we should be increasing what we owe and selling off everything that we own."

"Only if we want to go out of business and increase the cash on hand," Holmes corrected. "For the most part, businesses invest their cash in assets that will earn money, and borrow when leveraging will help them earn even more money. The caution is to remain liquid enough to pay regular expenses and meet emergencies.

"All right, that covers the purpose of the Cash Flow Statement and the ways in which we calculate increases and decreases in cash from the changes in the Income Statement and Balance Sheet. Let's briefly look at the way the Cash Flow Statement is organized before applying its data to FerMon."

The Main Divisions

"Notice that we begin with Net Income, which is taken directly from the Income Statement. As we have seen, that amount is calculated using the accrual method. The rest of the items on the Income Statement help us convert this figure into the net amount of cash that flowed in or out during the year."

"So the Net Cash Flow near the bottom on the sheet indicates that we had $109,000 less in cash than we had at the end of the previous year," Sue observed.

"Exactly. Now, if you look at the major divisions of the Cash Flow Statement, you will see there are four main calculations: we start with the Net Income and add back in the deductions that do not actually use cash, like depreciation, and then add the increases and subtract the decreases in cash from the company's three main activities: operations, investing, and financing."

Adding Depreciation Back in

"I don't see how Depreciation adds to our cash," Greg objected.

"It doesn't actually bring in money," Holmes agreed. "But if you look at the Income Statement, you'll see that we subtracted this amount as an expense when calculating the Net Income. Although depreciation is a tax deduction, it does not actually reduce our cash. So, when we are figuring what affects our supply of cash, we have to add this amount back in."

Accounting for Changes from Operations

"Operating cash flow is generated from internal operations—that is, from the sales of a business's products or services," Holmes pointed out. "It is the real lifeblood of a business, and because it is generated internally, it is under management's control."

"If sales are the source of operating profits, then why aren't they mentioned in the Operations section here?" Sue asked.

"As you know, we have already figured profits from sales in the Income Statement," Holmes answered. "That details both the income from sales and the expenses for labor, materials, utilities, maintenance, and every other item connected with making lamps and running the company."

"Okay," Greg pursued, "then why are operations mentioned here at all?"

"Because, on the Income Statement, the items for operations are recorded on an accrual basis. As we have already noted, increasing or decreasing the values of items like Inventory and Accounts Payable results in increases or decreases in cash. The Cash Flow Statement helps us see the cash impact of various accrual items."

Fixed Assets and Financing

"Since Fixed Assets are another kind of asset, I would imagine that the same logic would hold for them," Sue said. "Buying more uses up cash, selling some provides cash."

"Quite so," Holmes agreed.

"As I recall from our discussion of the Balance Sheet," Greg added, "borrowing money gives us cash, and paying off loans reduces cash, so our Notes Payable and Long-Term Debt entries are pretty obvious, too."

"While we are picking out the obvious things," Sue chimed in, "paying us dividends obviously reduces cash. I gather that this figure includes both what we're given for paying the taxes for the S Corporation and what is really income for us."

"Right again," Holmes commended them. "You can also see why, since you own the stock and none is for sale on the market, no cash is involved. However, I'd like you to consider what would happen to cash if the company were to issue more stock."

"Well," Greg thought out loud, "if it were sold, I suppose it would bring in cash, but if it were simply given away, say as bonuses to the management or employees, it would have no effect on cash."

"Of course, in the latter case, it would make our stock worth less," Sue added, "because we'd be sharing the ownership of the same assets."

Dividends as a Financing Activity

"One thing I don't understand is why Dividends are placed under Financing," Greg said. "How can paying out money and receiving nothing in return be considered an investment activity?"

"Can you see it as an investment activity for those who buy stock in a company?" Holmes asked.

"I guess so," Greg replied. "I mean, it doesn't seem immediately apparent to me because we've inherited the stock. But if one thinks of people buying stock, then dividends are a return on their investments."

"Right," Holmes agreed. "Now think of the company's point of view as the complement or mirror image of this: it receives the stockholders' investment and pays them a return. In a sense, it's a little like receiving a loan and paying interest for the use of the money."

The Five-Year Perspective

"All right," Holmes said as he spread out the five-year Cash Flow Statement. "It's time to see what these data tell us about FerMon.

(in thousands) **Statement of Cash Flows**					
	Year 1	Year 2	Year 3	Year 4	Year 5
Cash Flows from Operations:					
Net Income	10,402	14,568	17,036	5,311	2,308
Depreciation	2,285	2,429	2,684	2,609	2,651
Changes in:					
Accounts Receivable	(1,384)	(2,558)	(4,269)	(2,030)	(168)
Inventories	(1,243)	(2,494)	(2,595)	(2,517)	(664)
Prepaid Expenses	(106)	(192)	(1,032)	(279)	(229)
Other Assets	187	(2,954)	(726)	2,045	(637)
Accounts Payable	926	1,714	2,443	1,125	677
Accrued Expenses	194	332	66	158	(41)
Deferred Taxes	38	42	29	37	92
Net Cash Provided	11,299	10,887	13,636	6,459	3,989
Cash Flows from Investing:					
Purchase of Fixed Assets	(2,134)	(6,198)	(4,373)	(1,310)	(1,957)
Net Cash Used	(2,134)	(6,198)	(4,373)	(1,310)	(1,957)
Cash Flows from Financing:					
Change in Notes Payable	266	5,821	5,744	223	362
Change in Long Term Debt	(1,349)	1,303	(973)	(1,683)	(772)
Change in Common Stock	0	0	0	0	0
Payment of Dividends	(6,681)	(10,926)	(12,777)	(3,983)	(1,731)
Net Cash from Investing	(7,764)	(3,802)	(8,006)	(5,443)	(2,141)
Net Cash Flow	1,401	887	1,257	(294)	(109)
Cash at Beginning of Year	2,841	4,242	5,129	6,386	6,092
Cash at End of Year	4,242	5,129	6,386	6,092	5,983

"As Sue pointed out a little while ago, we had a negative cash flow of $109,000 last year," Holmes began.

"And an even bigger one of $294,000 the year before," Sue added.

Greg whistled. "That's $403,000! I was going to say that at least the flow slowed down last year, but then I noticed that we've helped that: our dividends went down by $2,000,000, but the flow only slowed down by $185,000."

"Good observations," Holmes commended them. "Can you see where the cash has gone?"

"Well, to begin with, the Net Cash Provided from Operations fell by two and a half million dollars last year," Sue observed. "And it fell by over seven million the year before that."

Holmes nodded. "Right. As we found out from the Balance Sheet and Income Statement, sales have fallen, our profit margin has shrunk, our inventory is swelling, and our short-term debts have been increasing. We have also seen disturbing increases in Accounts Payable and Accounts Receivable. The question here is, what new insights into the business can we glean from the Cash Flow Statement?"

The cousins studied the statement for several minutes.

Investment in Fixed Assets

"One thing that really looks different in this statement is the investment in fixed assets," Greg finally stated. "On the Balance Sheet, the steady growth in assets seems to chart a steady growth in the company's value. On the Cash Flow Statement, however, I see $16 million in cash going into Fixed Assets during the past five years, but our Net Income shrinking by $8 million from Year 1 and by almost $15 million from Year 3."

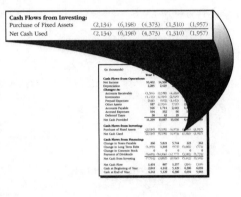

"You've hit on one of the biggest questions," Holmes complimented him. "Either we're not using the new resources in the right way, or they are a bad investment. They could be a bad investment because they are not suited to our needs or because we're facing new problems that can't be solved by new factories."

"Surely people still need lamps," Greg objected.

"But maybe a completely different type of lighting," Sue interposed.

"Or we may be facing new competition, like cheaper, imported lamps," Holmes added. "We need to find out what is happening. Ultimately, we might find out that selling these new assets could get rid of a problem. We might even find that, if new investments can't make us more competitive, we might need to consider selling the company while it still has value."

"I would hate for that to be the case," Sue commented.

"Me, too," Greg agreed.

"Naturally, that is a last recourse," Holmes said. "Nevertheless, one has to consider all sides of the question. But we're getting ahead of ourselves. Right now, we are framing questions for the management."

Borrowed Money

"Another thing I've noticed is that, aside from Net Income, our two main sources of cash last year were Accounts Payable and Note Payable," Sue continued.

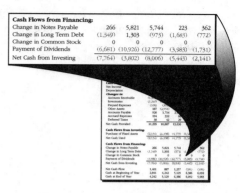

Cash Flows from Financing:					
Change in Notes Payable	266	5,821	5,744	223	362
Change in Long Term Debt	(1,349)	1,303	(973)	(1,683)	(772)
Change in Common Stock	0	0	0	0	0
Payment of Dividends	(6,681)	(10,926)	(12,777)	(3,983)	(1,731)
Net Cash from Investing	(7,764)	(3,802)	(8,006)	(5,443)	(2,141)

"Yeah, they provided over a million dollars," Greg concurred.

"In effect," Holmes added, "you can consider both of those sources to be borrowed money. We borrow from the bank or our suppliers. The growth in Accounts Payable could also lead to problems with our suppliers: if we take too long paying up, they may be reluctant to continue sending us new supplies."

Payments

"There is one other drain on cash I hate to bring up, but we have to look into everything," Holmes continued. "Look at the Dividends."

"I guess they were over 1.7 million dollars," Sue noted reluctantly. "But, after all, that includes the taxes for the S corporation, and it's only about 15% of what it was two years ago."

"There's truth in what you say," Holmes agreed. "Still, according to the Income Statement, $958,000 of that amount covered the taxes, leaving $773,000 as the effective payment to you and Greg. Given the negative cash flow of $109,000, that size payment doesn't seem justified since the company appears to have had to borrow money to pay your dividends."

"I suppose there's something to that," Greg conceded. "But we had Net Sales of almost $150 million last year. You'd think there'd be other reasonable places to save money."

"I hope there are," Holmes said. "Our questions will be directed at trying to find out how to improve the company's finances. Nevertheless, there is a need to keep a company profitable and solvent—in the sense of being able to pay bills as they come due. A key ingredient is maintaining a positive cash flow. If this hasn't occurred at the end of the year and there is no sound reason to expect significant improvements the next year, then cutting dividends is a responsible step to take."

The cousins did not look happy, but they nodded agreement.

"Certainly, keeping the company financially sound is the most important thing," Sue said. "I wouldn't want the company to have to sell profitable assets or start laying people off."

"Yes, keeping the company sound is in everyone's best long-term interests," Holmes said. "Now that we have covered the three major statements, we could put together our questions and get a good picture of the company's present condition. However, I'd first like to go over one final analysis that will help sharpen our understanding of the information we have already uncovered."

CHAPTER 10

Financial Ratios and Analysis Tools

Refined Figures

"It seems to me that we have already gained a pretty good picture of what's going on with the company," Greg observed. "Why do we need to go through yet another kind of analysis?"

"It's true that the Balance Sheet and the Income and Cash Flow Statements provide detailed information about a company," Holmes conceded. "Annual reports typically stop there, and relatively few people look any further. Nevertheless, just as the Cash Flow Statement helped us see some aspects of the company in a new light, so these additional calculations, based on figures from the other statements, will sharpen our understanding of specific strengths and weaknesses in the company."

"Judging from the items under 'Liquidity,' I'd say that section offers refinements of the Cash Flow Statement," Sue observed.

"That's basically right," Holmes agreed. "More specifically, it measures the company's ability to pay its bills as they come due. The 'Operating' section is a different look at the company's profitability."

"Since we're not looking at physical safety here, I assume that we're looking at financial soundness in the 'Safety and Leverage' section," Greg added.

"Yes. That section provides a slightly different point of view: how a banker might look at the company while deciding about extending a loan. Of course, we can look at that section to help us appraise the way the company is being financed and, thus, how sound it is."

Liquidity

"Now that seems a bit peculiar to me," Sue protested. "We seem to have plenty of assets, so why should there be any question of the company's financial soundness?"

"Remember the definition of 'liquidity': the ability to quickly turn assets into cash," Holmes reminded her. "If you loaned a friend a considerable amount of money for a short time, you would not want to hear that your being repaid would have to await the sale of a major asset like a home."

"That could take awhile," Greg agreed.

"For major loans, there is also the question of how much cash the quick sale of a fixed asset or an investment might bring," Holmes continued. "A lender might figure the collateral value on your cash at close to 100%, but as we move down the scale of liquidity, the percentage drops. Receivables might be valued at 70% to 80%, inventory at 60% to 70%, and fixed assets at only 40% to 50%."

"That seems rather unfair," Sue protested.

"That doesn't mean the lenders are buying the assets at this rate or forcing a company to sell at that rate," Holmes clarified. "It just indicates how much money they will extend based upon those assets as collateral or security for their loans. Of course, if a company can prove that particular assets are worth more—for example, that some property or machinery is in great demand—it can negotiate higher valuations."

The Liquidity Calculations

Holmes spread out two pages. "Here is a Financial Analysis based upon the information from several annual reports. I have added a copy of a chart I designed to show how these calculations are derived from the other parts of the annual report."

(in thousands) **Financial Analysis**	Year 1	Year 2	Year 3	Year 4	Year 5
Liquidity					
Current Ratio	1.82	1.52	1.43	1.50	1.49
Quick Ratio	1.06	0.88	0.84	0.85	0.83
Net Working Capital	16,411	14,556	15,545	18,724	18,748
Receivable Turn (Times)	7.54	7.92	7.55	6.26	5.70
Receivable Turn (Days)	48	46	48	58	64
Inventory Turn (Times)	6.16	6.28	5.95	5.23	4.64
Inventory Turn (Days)	59	58	61	70	79
Payable Turn (Times)	10.41	9.55	8.48	7.82	7.14
Payable Turn (Days)	35.06	38.20	43.05	46.66	51.13
Safety & Leverage					
Debt / Equity	0.92	1.08	1.14	1.10	1.10
EBIT / Interest	5.50	6.02	5.16	2.26	1.50
Dividend Payout	64.23%	75.00%	75.00%	75.00%	75.00%
Operating					
Sales Growth		14.87%	12.89%	-3.73%	-3.57%
EBITDA	14,998	19,899	23,819	12,126	9,546
Gross Margin	34.60%	35.60%	36.80%	32.96%	32.34%
Operating Margin	9.70%	11.84%	12.69%	5.96%	4.36%
Net Margin	8.10%	10.04%	10.39%	3.41%	1.56%
Return on Assets	16.18%	18.89%	19.21%	5.91%	2.54%
Return on Equity	31.04%	39.21%	41.14%	12.43%	5.33%

Financial Analysis

Item	Calculation
Liquidity	
Current Ratio	Current Assets / Current Liabilities
Quick Ratio	(Cash + Receivables) / Current Assets
Net Working Capital	Current Assets – Current Liabilities
Receivable Turn (Times)	Net Sales / Average[1] Accounts Receivable
Receivable Turn (Days)	365 / Receivable Turn (Times)
Inventory Turn (Times)	Cost of Goods Sold / Average[1] Inventory
Inventory Turn (Days)	365 / Inventory Turn (Times)
Payable Turn (Times)	Cost of Goods Sold / Accounts Payable
Payable Turn (Days)	365 / Payable Turn (Times)
Safety & Leverage	
Debt / Equity	Total Liability / Total Equity
EBIT / Interest	**I**ncome **B**efore **I**nterest and **T**axes / Interest
Dividend Payout	Tax and regular dividends / Income before Taxes
Operating	
Sales Growth	Current Gross Sales – preceding year's sales / preceding year's sales
EBITDA	Earnings Before Interest, Taxes, Depreciation, and Amortization
Gross Margin	Gross Profit / Net Sales
Operating Margin	Operating Income / Net Sales
Net Margin	Income before taxes / Net Sales
Return on Assets	Income before taxes / Total Assets
Return on Equity	Income before taxes / Total Equity

[1]To calculate the "average" Receivables or Inventory amount, add the figures for the current and preceding years and divide the result by 2.

Current and Quick Ratios

The cousins studied the two pages. Then Greg said, "I guess I understand the general idea of dividing Current Assets by Current Liabilities. It is another way of gauging how many liquid assets we have to cover our shorter-term bills."

"Having about 1.5 times as much sounds like an ample amount," Sue added.

"In this industry, we generally look for at least that amount," Holmes said. "Ideally, we would like a ratio of 2 to 1. However, a ratio of 1.5 to 1 does fall within acceptable limits by itself, and it has remained fairly steady on the FerMon statements during the past few years."

"One thing I question is the liquidity of the prepaid expenses, which are included under Current Assets," Greg objected.

"As I said earlier, lenders require greater amounts of collateral for the less liquid forms of assets," Holmes agreed. "That's why we prefer overall ratios of 2 to 1. A bigger potential problem, though, is the question of timing.

This ratio does not tell us when we will receive cash for the amounts in Receivables and Inventory, or when we will have to pay current bills. That is why this figure, by itself, doesn't tell us enough."

"Well, what about the Quick Ratio? It is Cash and Receivables divided by Current Liabilities," Sue observed. "I guess that tells us what percentage of our Current Liabilities is covered by our most liquid assets."

"They total 83%," Greg added, "which doesn't seem enough to pay bills without selling at least some Inventory."

"You've hit on our industry's ideal," Holmes replied, "a ratio of 1 to 1, or 100%. However, a ratio of 0.75 to 1, or 75%, is acceptable. As was the case with the Current Ratio, FerMon's Quick Ratio figure is somewhat on the low side but falls within the acceptable parameters. Note that the Quick Ratio statistic also ignores the timing of receipts and payments."

"Since the Quick Ratio deals only with Cash and Receivables, our most liquid assets, isn't the question of timing there less critical?" Sue asked.

"Good point," Holmes commended her. "But we still have to consider timing, especially since we have already noted growing delays in the payment of Receivables."

Industry Norms

"You have mentioned 'industry norms' a couple of times," Greg observed. "Do you mean that what is 'good' and 'bad' varies with the type of company?"

"Absolutely," Holmes replied. "For example, a company that services computers should have a lot less money tied up in inventory than an automobile dealer."

"But if there are no broad standards, how can one evaluate the financial-analysis figures in an annual report?" Sue asked.

"That's not always easy," Holmes admitted. "You would start with the trade association and publications dedicated to a particular industry. You could also access the Annual Statement Studies, available through RMA (The Risk Management Association) at www.rmahq.org for information on a number of industries."

Net Working Capital

Greg scratched his head. "I'm a little confused by the term 'Working Capital.' I thought all the money invested in a company was working capital."

Holmes smiled. "In a broad sense, I suppose it is. More precisely, Working Capital is that part of the overall capital invested in Current Assets. These investments generally turn over many times a year—hence the term 'Working' Capital. This is in contrast to more long-term investments like Fixed Assets. To calculate the Net Working Capital, subtract Current Liabilities from Current Assets."

"I see," Sue nodded. "You figure that the amount we currently owe determines how much of our current assets we need to keep handy. By subtracting that amount, we have a fairly good estimate of how much of the current assets can be used for other purposes."

"Exactly. Now, according to the figure for last year, we have almost $19 million of Net Working Capital. Does that sound like a good amount?"

"It would be a fabulous amount for a neighborhood business, but a totally inadequate amount for a Fortune 500 company," Greg replied.

"Excellent," Holmes beamed. "In order to make the number more meaningful for our company, we have to look at the Current and Quick Ratios. For example, the Current Ratio tells us that we have $1.49 in Current Assets for every $1 of Current Liability. That means that we could liquidate our Current Assets for as little as 71¢ on the dollar and still be able to pay our current creditors."

Receivable Turns

"We have already seen how Accounts Receivable has been growing," Holmes continued. "This means that customers are taking longer to pay us. If the average amount in Receivables were equal to half the amount of our Net Sales, then we would say that the Receivables are paid up, or 'turn over,' only twice a year, and that our customers were taking an average of six months to pay us. If Receivables were a quarter of the amount of Net Sales, then we would have four turns per year, and our customers would be taking an average of three months to pay us."

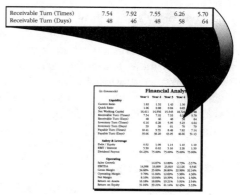

"How do you come up with an 'average' figure for Receivables?" Greg asked. "Do you dig up the monthly figures?"

"That would be an accurate way," Holmes admitted, "but we usually settle for a shortcut: add together the amount at the beginning of the year and that for the end of the year, and divide that total by two."

"Where do you see the amount for the beginning of the year—oh, wait, I remember," Sue exclaimed. "The amount at the end of one year is the same as the amount for the beginning of the next."

"All right," Holmes continued, "by dividing the average Receivables amount into Net Sales, we get the number of turns in a year. Obviously, the more turns, the better. In our industry, we should see about 9 turns a year."

"Well, the report never shows anything that good," Greg sighed. "The best was about 7.9 in Year Two, and the number of turns has fallen to 5.7 for last year."

"We can see this in an even more vivid way by dividing the number of days in a year by the number of turns," Holmes pointed out. "The 7.9 turns in Year Two mean an average collection time of 46 days, whereas last year's 5.7 turns mean the collection time has grown to 64 days. In contrast, the industry norm of 9 turns translates into a collection time of under 41 days."

"I think we have already brought up some possible causes of this lengthening payment time," Sue said. "We may have extended our trade terms and taken on shakier customers in order to sell more lamps. And we may simply need better collection practices."

"And there may be a connection with the increases in Warranty Expense, Returns and Allowances, and Scrap," Greg added. "I believe we said poorer quality could be causing customer dissatisfaction, which could mean our customers are withholding payment until their complaints have been settled."

"You're both right about the possible causes, though we need more information from the management to be sure," Holmes said. "The effects are more certain: an increase in collection time adds days to our cash cycle and requires more resources. According to the Cash Flow Statement, the Receivables have grown by $10 million during the past five years, which means they tie up an additional $10 million in cash. This might be healthy if we were supporting profitable growth, but it is not healthy when sales and profits are decreasing."

Inventory Turns

"I suppose inventory turns means how many times we sell the Inventory in a year," Sue commented. "I'm not sure how you derive this by dividing the Cost of Goods Sold by the average Inventory."

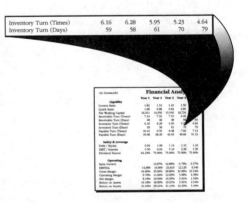

| Inventory Turn (Times) | 6.16 | 6.28 | 5.95 | 5.23 | 4.64 |
| Inventory Turn (Days) | 59 | 58 | 61 | 70 | 79 |

"As you may recall from the Income Statement," Holmes answered, "the Cost of Goods Sold is our manufacturing costs, such as labor, materials, and factory overhead, but not our administration and sales costs. These manufacturing costs are the same ones we use when computing the Inventory. So, dividing the year's Cost of Goods Sold by the average amount in Inventory shows us how many times Inventory has to be sold in order to reach the year's total."

"This doesn't look so good, either," Greg noted. "We have gone from about 6.3 turns in Year Two to 4.6 turns last year. I'm almost afraid to ask what the industry norm is."

"The norm is about 8 times per year," Holmes said.

"Dividing 4.7 turns into 365 gives us about 79 days as the length of time goods stay in Inventory," Sue noted.

"And dividing 365 days by the industry norm of 8 turns gives us a normal turnover time of about 46 days," Greg calculated. "That's quite a difference!"

"Yes," Holmes agreed. "According to the Cash Flow Statement, we see that Inventory increases have required additional cash of almost $10 million over the past five years. Management should be making serious attempts to control the inventory better by making sure it is all usable and consists of products that are currently in demand. It may also want to make sure we are not ordering excessive raw materials."

"If Inventory and the Cost of Goods Sold take in all manufacturing costs, should we be addressing those costs as well?" Sue asked.

"Absolutely," Holmes replied. "Management should make sure our labor and overhead costs sure under control. A look at our Operating Ratios will help clarify whether we have efficiency problems as well."

Payable Turns

"I'm a bit confused about this next one," Greg confessed. "Your guide sheet says we divide the Cost of Goods Sold by the average Accounts Payable. But I don't see a tight relationship between the two: the Cost of Goods Sold includes things like labor and factory maintenance as well as raw materials, and Accounts Payable includes not only the costs of raw materials but everything else we buy, including supplies and services for the administrative offices."

Payable Turn (Times)	10.41	9.55	8.48	7.82	7.14
Payable Turn (Days)	35.06	38.20	43.05	46.66	51.13

"That's why we have to compare our findings with the industry norms," Holmes explained. "In a wholesale or retail company, for example, the Cost of Goods Sold would be pretty much the same as what it pays its suppliers, and most of its Accounts Payable would also be for its suppliers."

"Last year, our Accounts Payable turned over about 7 times, for an average of 51 days," Sue noted. "How does that compare with our industry norms?"

"The industry norm is about 15 turns a year, or an average of about 24 days."

The cousins whistled. "That's less than half the time we're taking!" Greg exclaimed.

"There are two other disturbing things," Sue added. "During the past five years, we have gone down from 10.4 turns and 35 days, which means we are taking half again as long to pay our bills. And that 'high point' of five years ago was still only 70% of the industry standard."

"Good observations," Holmes nodded. "This would seem to indicate the company is having cash-flow problems and is borrowing from its suppliers as well as from the banks. This could also be lead to problems with the suppliers."

"Is it also possible that we have gone to poorer-quality suppliers who are more willing to extend credit?" Greg asked. "That could tie in with our quality problems."

"It is a legitimate question to ask," Holmes agreed, "though right now, that is highly conjectural. A more certain effect is that it is forcing us to pay more for our raw materials, which could be a factor in our increasing inventory costs and lower profitability. Again, though, we need more information before we can responsibly entertain such theories."

Cash Cycle

"There is one further calculation that we can make from these turns figures," Holmes pointed out. "If it normally takes us 79 days to sell our inventory and another 64 days to collect our Receivables for those sales, then we have to wait 143 days from the time we buy our raw materials to when we collect the cash for the sale of our finished product. This is referred to as a Cash Cycle."

The cousins studied the statement for a few moments, and then Sue said, "In Year Two, the Cash Cycle was only 104 days, so our present figure of 143 days is about 38% longer."

"If I remember right," Greg added, "we are carrying about $20 million more in Inventory and Accounts Receivable now, so we are financing more money for a longer period of time."

"That's true," Holmes agreed. "The increases in these assets would have been okay in Years One and Three, when sales were up, but are increasingly problematical now that sales and profits have gone down during the past two years."

Sue continued staring at the Financial Analysis statement. "Wait a minute. What about Accounts Payable? If we're not paying our suppliers as soon as we receive our raw materials, then we're not carrying all this financing for the full length of the Cash Cycle you mentioned."

"That's true," Holmes conceded. "Since our suppliers are now carrying our raw-material costs for 51 days, we can subtract that time from 143 to obtain our true Cash Cycle of 92 days. The average for the industry is 40 days for Receivables, 45 days for Inventory, and 24 days for Payables resulting in a 61-day Cash Cycle. That still leaves our Cash Cycle about 50% longer than the industry standard. If we were paying our suppliers in line with the industry average of 24 days, our Cash Cycle would be 119 days, or about double the industry norm."

Sue snapped her fingers. "We have also increased our Cash Cycle from 66 days in Year Two to the current 92 days in Year Five. That is practically the same percent increase as we came up with when we figured the changes in the Cash Cycle without figuring in the lag in Accounts Payable."

"Hmm," Greg muttered. "I can see where more statistics give us a more complete picture of the company. Although our Net Working Capital, Current Ratio, and Quick Ratio do not appear to signal any fundamental problems, the turns ratios indicate major difficulties with liquidity."

Safety and Leverage

"The 'Safety and Leverage' ratios give us additional insights into a business's vulnerability to risk," Holmes noted. "These ratios are often used by creditors to determine the ability of a business to repay loans."

Safety & Leverage					
Debt / Equity	0.92	1.08	1.14	1.10	1.10
EBIT / Interest	5.50	6.02	5.16	2.26	1.50
Dividend Payout	64.23%	75.00%	75.00%	75.00%	75.00%

"What do you mean by 'vulnerability to risk'?" Sue asked.

"It takes in quite a few things," Holmes answered. "To put it simply: the less a company owes and the more it owns, the better it is able to meet unexpected challenges like sudden downturns in the economy and emergencies requiring sizable expenditures."

Debt to Equity

"Dividing our total debt by our total equity gives us a view of the relative financing from the owners and lenders," Holmes said.

"I suppose lenders want to see a high ratio of owner equity," Greg opined.

"Of course," Holmes agreed. "However, looking at this from the owner's point of view, too little debt can also signal a problem. Remember our discussion of leveraging: failure to use borrowed money can slow a company's growth. Larger public companies have to bear in mind that their shareholders want their riskier investment to be rewarded with a higher dividend rate or growth in stock value than they can obtain by the safer strategy of putting their money into a bank account or bonds."

"So how do we measure up to our industry's norm on this ratio?" Sue asked.

"Our industry shows an average Debt to Equity Ratio of about 1.7 to 1," Holmes replied. "Thus, our ratio of 1.1 to 1 shows less debt and higher ownership than the industry averages."

Interest-Coverage Ratio or Times-Interest-Earned Ratio

"This seems pretty straightforward," Sue remarked. "How much of our earnings goes to paying interest."

"Yes, or, as the lenders look at it, whether the profits are strong enough to pay the interest without the need for liquidating other assets," Holmes added.

"Offhand, I'd say this is one of the most disturbing figures we've come across yet," Greg commented. "Last year the ratio was only 1.5, which means two-thirds of our profits are going into paying interest. This reminds me of the people who are barely keeping up with their credit-card charges."

"Industry averages are difficult to find in this area," Holmes said, "but an average coverage of about 4 times would be considered safe in normal circumstances."

"Then Year Two's ratio of 6 times as much income as interest payments was quite impressive," Sue commented. "The rapid decline to 1.5 sounds like a key question for the management."

Dividend Payout Ratio

"Okay, here's one you may not like to consider, but it is important," Holmes cautioned.

"The dividends can't be that big a factor," Greg objected. "According to the figures on the Income Statement, last year we received less than 15% as much as we did in Year Three."

"That's true in absolute figures," Holmes conceded. "However, we need to evaluate dividends in relation to profits. This ratio tells us how much a company can responsibly afford to pay out as dividends."

"Are you lumping together the 'dividends' we receive to pay the taxes and the real dividends we get to keep?" Sue asked.

"Partially," Holmes admitted. "This ratio is derived by dividing the net profits before taxes into the total dividends, but we also make some separate calculations."

"I would think that industry figures on this would be as confidential and difficult to obtain as the interest figures we just talked about," Greg remarked.

"That's true," Holmes replied. "We can, however, take 40% as a typical figure that S corporations pay as tax dividends. We cannot settle upon a comparable norm for the 'Other Dividends' category, but we can make some meaningful observations from the FerMon statements."

"The statement says that the company has been paying out 75% of the profits for dividends," Sue observed. "Does that mean that our much smaller 'Other' dividend represents 35% of the profits? I assume you would subtract the 40% tax figure from the combined 75% figure."

"That's exactly right," Holmes replied. "In Year One, the company had paid out 64% of net income or about 24% beyond the 40% tax dividend, and this increased to 75% in Year Two, when profits soared. Since then, though profits have fallen sharply, the company has continued paying out the combined total of 75% in dividends. Given the shrinking ratio of profits to interest payments, lenders will probably not be happy about this, especially if the company has to restructure its debts."

"So you're saying we should have our 'Other' dividend reduced even more," Greg concluded.

"Or even eliminated until profits improve and the ratio between profits and interest payments improves significantly," Holmes agreed.

"Well," Sue frowned, "I guess we could endure that so long as this led to the longer-term improvement in the company."

Greg pursed his lips and nodded agreement. "After all, we have a lot of money tied up in the company. It wouldn't make sense to risk all that for the sake of a few short-term dividends."

Operating Ratios

"This final, 'Operating,' section gives us some added insights into the company's ability to make a profit and its performance as an investment," Holmes said.

Operating					
Sales Growth		14.87%	12.89%	-3.73%	-3.57%
EBITDA	14,998	19,899	23,819	12,126	9,546
Gross Margin	34.60%	35.60%	36.80%	32.96%	32.34%
Operating Margin	9.70%	11.84%	12.69%	5.96%	4.36%
Net Margin	8.10%	10.04%	10.39%	3.41%	1.56%
Return on Assets	16.18%	18.89%	19.21%	5.91%	2.54%
Return on Equity	31.04%	39.21%	41.14%	12.43%	5.33%

Sales Growth

"Seeing how sales are increasing is obviously important," Sue remarked. "I suppose one could measure this in many ways."

"Yes," Holmes agreed. "This way is the most common: take the difference between this year's sales and last year's, and divide the result by last year's. That tells us the increase as a percentage of the previous year's sales. If sales increased from, to take an easy number, $1,000,000 last year to $1,100,000 this year, we'd say that they had increased by 10%."

"And if they went down to $900,000, I suppose we'd say that they had decreased by 10%," Greg added.

"Exactly," Holmes concurred. "Unfortunately, decreases of 3.7% and 3.6% are what we see for the past two years in the FerMon report. Contrast that with the period from Year One to Year Three, when sales grew nicely."

"What is a normal increase in sales?" Sue asked.

"Other than saying one looks for steady increases in sales, that is hard to answer," Holmes replied. "Certainly we want to see sales match our overall costs and inflation, which can vary greatly. We also need to look at the overall market conditions: whether we are at least keeping pace with the total market's sales in lamps. If everybody's sales are down, we would at least expect our sales to be down no more than the average amount, and hopefully be down less."

"Wouldn't it be possible to increase profits even if sales were down—say, by cutting costs or selling a lot fewer low-margin lamps but increasing the sales of those with higher profit margins?" Greg asked.

"Yes," Holmes agreed. "That is why we have to look at our profitability as well as at raw sales. We also need to estimate how much lower sales could go before we begin to lose money. We can do this by calculating our Break-Even point."

Break-Even Analysis

"Isn't the break-even point where you sell a product for exactly what it cost you to make it?" Sue asked. "For example, if a store bought a lamp for $100 and sold it for the same amount, it would break even."

"In a way," Greg rejoined. "However, doesn't the store have to handle other expenses, like processing the purchase and sale, and paying its heat, rent, and employees?"

"That's true," Sue admitted. "But how do you factor in all those costs?"

Holmes flipped to a blank page on the flip chart, then sketched the following diagram:

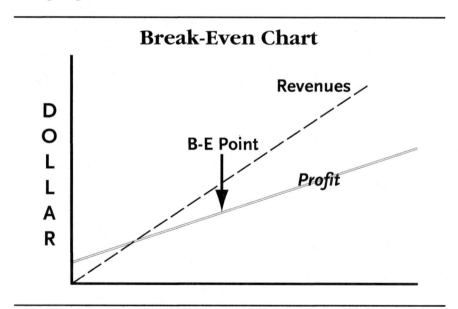

"As you've pointed out, because of the number of variable factors, this calculation will be an approximation," Holmes said. "Nevertheless, it is very useful for evaluating our present situation and planning for the future. Let's start with the easiest part, the Fixed Costs, which my example equates with operating expenses. These are items like administrative costs, rent for the office, office equipment, telephone, heat, and so on—things we have to pay whether we manufacture twice as many lamps or none at all. Obviously, we have to sell enough lamps for more than their manufacturing cost to pay these Fixed Costs. I should point out that some costs in this area, like Sales Commissions, should be included in Variable Costs."

"By elimination, then, Variable Costs must cover items that vary with how much we sell," Greg opined.

"That makes sense," Sue added. "That would take in items like raw materials and wages paid for manufacturing the products that were sold."

"Certainly," Holmes agreed. "As we make more lamps, we have to buy more raw materials and add workers or pay overtime."

"This is getting more complicated by the minute," Greg moaned. "By emphasizing 'products sold,' I take it that we don't count the costs of manufacturing the products that are still in the inventory."

"We're going to simplify it now," Holmes reassured him. "Since operating expenses other than Cost of Goods Sold do not generally fluctuate with each item sold, we will refer to these expenses as Fixed. As to figuring Variable Costs, since Cost of Goods Sold relates directly to the sales of our products, we can look at them as Variable Costs. Do you remember when we talked about the Contribution Margin in connection with the Income Statement?"

The cousins referred to the Income Statement. Then Sue said, "I believe we calculated the Contribution Margin by subtracting the Cost of Goods Sold from the Net Sales."

"That's right," Greg chimed in. "The Cost of Goods Sold represents our production costs, which are variable. Anything we make above that goes toward paying the Fixed Costs and earning profits."

"That's it," Holmes nodded. "Last year, our Net Sales were about $148 million, and our Cost of Sales was about $100 million. Dividing $100 million by $148 million tells us that the Cost of Sales was about 68% of our selling price. That means that our Contribution Margin is 32%. Put another way, for every dollar of sales, 68 cents goes to pay for making the product, our Variable Cost, and 32 cents goes towards paying our Fixed Expenses. Only after they are paid can we be said to have made a profit."

"So, in your example, the Fixed Costs are the same as the Operating Expenses on the Income Statement?" Greg asked.

"Yes. Our immediate question, then, is the minimum amount we have to sell in order to pay our Fixed Costs. Again, to start with a simple figure, to earn $100 above our Variable Costs, we have to sell more than $300 dollars in lamps, because every $100 in sales gives us only $32 beyond the $68 that goes toward the Variable, or manufacturing, Costs. More precisely, $100 divided by 0.32 tells us we need $312.50 in sales to earn $100 towards our Fixed Costs. You can check this out: $0.32 times $312.50 equals $100."

The cousins pondered this for a moment. Then Sue punched some numbers into the calculator. "Let's see, then: to figure how much in Sales is needed to meet the Fixed, or Operating, Costs of $41 million, we divide that by $0.32, which give us $128,125,000."

"Very good," Holmes smiled. "That is our Break-Even number for last year."

"You said this calculation can be used for planning," Greg said. "Do you mean that we can use this for setting goals?"

"Of course," Holmes replied. "But it is much more flexible than that. For example, we can calculate the effects of making changes to our operations. If we cut our Fixed Costs, we lower our Break-Even Point. We can also lower it by increasing our Contribution Margin, by lowering our Cost of Goods Sold, or by selling more items on which we earn a higher profit. Conversely, if we increase our Fixed Costs or lower our Contribution Margin, we will need more sales just to break even."

"I see," Sue nodded. "If we lowered our Operating Costs to, say, $38 million, we would be dividing that figure by $0.32, and if we increased our Contribution Margin to, say, $0.35, we would divide by that figure, which would give us a lower Break-Even Point."

"That's right. We can also use the Break-Even calculation to help us determine what sales we need to provide a specific return to shareholders. Let's say that we want an industry average of 8% Return on Equity from our company. Since our Equity at the end of Year Five was approximately $43,000,000, that means we would need 8% of that number in profits before taxes, or $ 3,440,000. If we add that profit figure to the Fixed-Cost figure, we would then divide the result, $44,440,000, by $0.32. That gives us $138,875,000, which is the amount of sales we would need to both pay our Fixed Cost of $41 million and make a profit of $3,440,000."

Greg scratched his head. "I have to confess that this kind of facile projection always makes me uneasy. It assumes an awful lot, like our Fixed Costs remaining the same."

"That's true," Holmes said. "However, no one has a crystal ball with a clear view of the future. Unless we see factors that will cause great changes, the best we can do is start with the present actual numbers and project them into the future. As things change, we change our projections."

"Did you say there were other ways of using these calculations?" Sue asked.

"Yes. We can use this formula to play 'what if' in a number of areas, from pricing and product mix to cost reductions and labor negotiations. This is a very helpful tool for management in forecasting the impact of various strategies."

EBITDA (Earnings Before Interest, Taxes, Depreciation, and Amortization)

"Wow, that EBITDA is a real mouthful!" Greg exclaimed.

"Yes, but the idea is pretty simple," Holmes rejoined. "This is a rough calculation of operating cash flow. As its name states, it is calculated by taking Net Profit before Taxes and adding back Interest expenses, Depreciation, and Amortization."

"I remember about depreciation's not being an actual payment in cash," Sue remarked. "I don't remember any 'Amortization' item on the other statements."

"Actually, 'amortization' can refer to a number of things," Holmes explained. "The general idea is that Amortization is similar to Depreciation but applies to Other Assets such as Goodwill and patents rather than to Fixed Assets.

"I think you can see why the sheer ability to generate cash is used by many as a key to evaluating a company as a financial investment. A company with a consistent growth will be evaluated at a premium by financial analysts."

"Even if most of that cash ends up going to pay interest on large debts?" Sue demanded.

"You're right: EBITDA does not tell us how well the management is using or financing the assets."

"Even so," Greg added, "the big declines in this figure during the past two years would seem to indicate trouble. The funny thing is, if we were examining the annual report at the end of Year Three, we would have seen big increases that would have marked this company as a good investment."

"That's true, and it tells us not to base our conclusions on just one or two figures. The way companies' fortunes can change is the reason for the warning on all investment prospectuses: 'Past performance is no guarantee of future earnings.' Even so, these kinds of projections are one of the major tools we have, and they are measurably better than flipping a coin or relying on the impulse of the moment. As we examine more figures, we improve our odds of making sound decisions."

Margin Analysis

Greg looked over the remaining entries. "Are the 'Gross' and 'Operating' Margins related to the Gross Profit and Operating Income entries on the Income Statement?"

Holmes nodded. "We simply divide those figures from the Income Statement by the Net Sales figure to see what percentages of profit we are gaining from the sales."

"What about the 'Net Margin'?" asked Sue. "There are two 'Net Income' figures on the Income Statement."

"We take the Net Income before Taxes," Holmes replied. "We generally want to see how effectively a company is performing, and taxes are imposed from without. Though a change in the tax rates would affect the Net Income after Taxes line, the change would not indicate that the company was performing any better or any worse."

Gross Margin

"Okay, so dividing the Gross Profit by the Net Sales gives us a Gross Margin of about 32%," Sue observed. "How does this stack up to the average for our industry?"

"32% is the industry average," Holmes replied. "Our figure for last year was, to be precise, 32.34%, or slightly above average."

"I suppose that's encouraging," Greg commented. "However, it can't be good that this percentage is the lowest it has been in five years, and was 36.8% only two years ago."

"You're right, one looks at trends, not just the absolute figure for the current year," Holmes agreed. "A shrinking margin here could mean that we are not getting as good prices for our products, our manufacturing costs are increasing faster than we can raise prices, or we are selling less of our more profitable items. With falling profit margins, the only way to make the same Gross Profit is to increase sales, but this has not happened."

"Couldn't we make up for the margin here by lowering our fixed costs?" Sue asked.

"One can improve the Net Profits that way," Holmes admitted. "However, a good Gross Margin is the best foundation for profits, since the Operating and Net profits come from this margin."

Operating Margin

"Continuing the same type of calculation, I assume we obtain the Operating Margin by dividing the Operating Income by the Net Sales," Greg stated.

"I suppose this tells us how efficient our administration is?" Sue added.

"In part," Holmes replied. "More precisely, it tells us about the company's profitability in its overall operations. "Remember, improvement in the Gross Margin or in sales will improve this line as well."

"Since Operating Expenses, or Fixed Costs, are relatively stable, then higher sales should mean better Operating Margins," Greg commented. "On the other hand, since Manufacturing Costs, or Variable Costs, vary according to how much we produce, theoretically the Gross Margin should remain about the same regardless of sales. If our pricing keeps up with our Cost of Goods Sold and if we continue selling the same mixture of cheaper and more expensive products, then our Gross Margin should not vary much. However, if our sales drop but our fixed expenses remain the same, I imagine that our Operating Margin would drop sharply."

"Generally the Gross Margin will not vary as much as the Operating

Margin," Holmes agreed. "When sales drop, the Operating Margin should drop as well. You can see that, whereas the Gross Margin dropped by about 4.5% between Years Three and Five, the Operating Margin dropped by over 12%. Even if we blame part of that 12% drop to the 4.5% drop in Gross Margin, you can see that most of the 12% drop has to be attributed to other causes."

"That 12% drop does sound bad," Sue agreed. "How does our Operating Margin compare to the industry norm?"

"That would be about 6.5%," Holmes replied. "So we have gone from 12.7%, almost double the norm, to 4.4%, about two-thirds the norm."

"So the ideal solution would be to increase sales?" Greg asked.

"Yes. Another good way would be to increase our profit margin, either by lowering our manufacturing costs or by selling a higher percentage of products with bigger profit margins."

"And if we can't do either?" Sue asked.

"Then we would have to find a way of reducing the Fixed Expenses," Holmes answered. "A few parts of it, like sales commissions, would go down automatically, and one can spend less on a few items like advertising. These do not amount to very much, however, so we would have to find ways of operating more efficiently or of cutting costs."

"Does that mean laying off people?" Greg frowned.

"It could," Holmes admitted. "Or not hiring additional people to replace those who leave. It can mean cutting back raises, using less expensive supplies and services. There are many ways. The point is, though the management has cut these costs a little, it needs to do more to stop this rapid shrinking of our Operating Margin."

Net Margin

"I would imagine that dividing the Net Profit before Taxes by Net Sales would tell us about our ultimate profitability," Sue opined.

"That's right," Holmes concurred. "And, before you ask, the average Net Margin in our industry was about 5.2%, which means that on average companies in our industry made a profit of only 5.2¢ for each dollar of product they sold."

"That doesn't sound very impressive," Greg commented. "Still, it looks a lot better than the 2¢ we made last year."

"Let me make sure I understand this correctly," Sue said. "It cost us 68¢ to make the products, and 30¢ to sell them and run the office, which leaves just 2¢ for reinvesting in the company and paying dividends?"

"That means we actually paid more of each sales dollar for interest on our loans than we received as shareholders," Greg added.

"That pretty much sums it up," Holmes agreed. "As is predictable from the declines in the Gross and Operating Margins, the Net Margin has declined from over 10% in Years Three to last year's 1.6%. This dramatic decline is partly attributable to the reduced sales levels and partly to very poor cost controls within the company. What we cannot determine without further information is the extent to which pricing and the mix of products sold have contributed to these declines."

Sue frowned. "Now that I think of it, even an average of 5.2% doesn't seem all that impressive. There must be safer investments that can bring that kind of return. Why do people work hard and take risks in business for this kind of return?"

"Partly for the hope of doing better," Holmes explained. "However, you cannot fully compare Net Income with, say, a savings account or a bond. Let's say you had a small store that sold $10,000 worth of inventory a week for a Net Income of 2%. At the end of the year, your books would show that you have bought and sold $520,000 worth of inventory at that same 2% margin, or $10,400. As you said, this would not seem worth the investment."

"How could it be?" Sue demanded.

"Because, if you think about it, you are using that same $10,000 every week," Holmes pointed out. "On the books, every time you restock, you are spending additional money, but with this rapid turnover of inventory, you are, in effect, doing this with a small amount of money. Thus, your $10,000 is earning you $10,400 a year."

Greg's eyes brightened. "So that gives a deeper meaning to Inventory Turns."

"Exactly. That's why we have to keep looking at all the important figures."

Return on Assets (ROA)

"The final two ratios measure how effectively the company is using its assets," Holmes said. "As Greg pointed out earlier, how good or bad a given amount of money is depends upon the size of the company. One can look at assets in two ways. First, we can estimate how well the management is using everything a company has, including assets financed by borrowing. Second, we can consider how good a return the shareholders are receiving for their investment."

After looking at the statement for a moment, Sue said, "So we divide the Net Profits before Taxes by the Total Assets—everything the company has use of—and this tells us how well the management is using those assets."

"Wow! The Return has gone down from 19.2% to about 2.5%!" Greg exclaimed. "It's hard to believe things could decline so much in just two years."

"Yes, and I can't think that 2.5% is a good figure, especially when I compare it to the first three years," Sue added.

"The industry average is about 8.8%," Holmes said. "As we noted in the Balance Sheet, the company invested heavily in a new plant in Year Two. Given the declines in sales during the past three years, we would have to say that the management has not made a good use of this new resource."

Return on Equity

"If I remember right, Equity is what the shareholders have invested in the company," Sue said.

"Yes, it is a combination of the stockholders' original investment plus all the Retained Earnings that have been kept for expanding the company," Holmes explained.

"So this figure looks at the company from the investors' point of view?" Greg asked.

"That's a good way of putting it," Holmes agreed. "When we divide Net Profit before Taxes by Equity, we are seeing what percent return you are getting for your investment dollar. You can compare this to the rate you might receive for a bank certificate of deposit, bonds, or other investments."

"I thought that increases in the value of the stock could serve as the main investment reward," Sue objected.

"That could be true of publicly traded stocks," Holmes agreed. "However, since your stocks are not being traded, this Return on Equity is based on their Book Value as opposed to Market Value."

"Since we don't buy and sell our stock, it is difficult for me to see this as a typical investment," Greg admitted.

"Look at it this way," Holmes suggested. "We can finance an expansion in several ways. You could invest more money, or we could go public and have new shareholders invest their money. We have seen the increasing pressure caused by the new loans from the past four years. If you or new shareholders invest money, the management would feel additional pressure to reward these riskier investments with higher Returns on Equity."

"I suppose so," Sue conceded. "So how high a return do investors typically get?"

"Our industry shows an average Return on Equity of about 26%," Holmes replied.

"Another bad figure for us," Greg observed. "Our return for last year was 5.33%, down from a high of over 41% in Year Three."

"Yes, given the risk factors of doing business in our industry, the 5.33% return does not appear to be acceptable," Holmes said. "Note, too, that during Years One through Three, we made very good profits and reinvested most of them in the company. As the shareholders, you deferred enjoying those profits in the expectation that the new investments would pay even bigger dividends in the future."

Chapter 11

Aftermath

Holmes flipped to a fresh page on the flip chart. "So, do you have a clearer picture of what's happening at FerMon?"

After thinking for a few moments, Greg began, "Well, not everything's bleak. For example, the assets of the company and our equity have grown considerably over the past five years, and there is a healthy ratio between the assets and our debts. We've also been paying down our long-term debt."

"I suppose this means, at a minimum, that if we had to sell out, we could pay all our creditors and still wind up with a decent amount of money," Sue added. "Not, of course, that this is what we want to do."

"Of course not," Holmes nodded as he finished putting these "pluses" on the chart. "Now, what apparent problems have we uncovered?"

"The ones that concern me the most are the drop in sales and the even more dramatic drop in profits," Greg replied. "If you can't make money, you can't solve any other problems."

"Yes, that is the central issue," Holmes agreed. "For example, we saw how the Operating Expenses have grown by almost $10 million. That wasn't a problem when the sales and profits were climbing even faster, but it is now that profits have shrunk."

"Another thing that bothers me is the apparent jump in quality problems," Sue said. "We saw that in entries like the increases expenses in entries like Returns and Allowances, Warranty Coverage, and Scrap."

"And don't forget the growth in Inventory," Greg added. "That, the decline in Sales, and the increased days for Receivable Turns also suggest problems with the quality or at least attractiveness of our lamps."

"Good," Holmes approved as he jotted these items on the chart. "What about the new plant?"

"Well," Sue replied, "when I came here today, I was concerned about its possible sale because I thought it was our principle source of new sales. Now that I see how much money has gone into it, how profits have fallen, and how quality problems have risen, I'm not so sure this is a good use of assets."

"Right, we'll have questions about this," Holmes agreed. "Anything else?"

"The main thing that comes to mind is the growing problem of cash flow," Greg commented. "Many of the things we've already mentioned, like shrinking profits, growing inventory, and lengthening receivables times, contribute to this. Another factor is our mounting short-term debt."

"Excellent!" Holmes approved. "We could bring in many more details, but I think this gives a pretty good overall picture. What questions does this raise for the management?"

"Well, if falling sales and profits are the central issues," Sue replied, "then we need to know why this is happening. Does it reflect an industry-wide problem, or are old or new competitors taking business away from us?"

"Yes, and what are the reasons for our growing inventory—are customers viewing our lamps as being poorer-quality, overpriced, or unfashionable?" Greg added.

"Good questions," Holmes nodded. "The question of stiffening competition also raises the unpleasant but necessary question of our long-term viability: can we fix the problems and prosper once again, or must we consider moving to a less expensive area or even selling our part or all of the business while it still has market value?"

The cousins looked uncomfortable. Then Sue said, "I guess we do have to consider all sides of the question. I'd like to make sure we consider all of the possible fixes. Certainly, improving sales and profit margins would be the ideal solution. Besides solving any quality or styling problems, we could also look into cutting expenses, like the Operating Expenses that went up almost $10 million."

"And what about all that short-term debt?" Greg added. "I would like to see it paid off fast, because that would save us a lot of interest over the long term. However, changing it to long-term debt would certainly help ease the cash-flow problem."

"Yes, we need to find out why the management hasn't made this switch," Holmes concurred. "It is possible that the banks are either unwilling to extend us long-term loans or are demanding substantially higher terms for doing so. Finding out what's behind this could give us new information about the company's financial soundness."

The cousins pondered the chart, looked at each other, then turned to Holmes.

"Well, Mr. Holmes," Sue said, "I suppose we could go back over many of the details we've covered, but I think this is a good summary. We seem to be in pretty good shape for meeting with the management and find out what's going on."

"Yeah," Greg smiled, "I guess understanding all those funny little terms can help make us more responsible owners."

CHAPTER 12

The Next Steps

"Whew!" said Sue as she and her cousin left Bob Holmes's office. "We need to talk."

"We sure do," Greg agreed. "Got some time now? We could get some lunch at Harry's Grill."

"Sounds good."

Thinking about all the information they had to digest, both were silent as Greg drove them to Harry's. Once in a booth, after a waitress took their order, however, they couldn't stop talking.

"I wish I had started raising these questions earlier," said Sue. "In fact, I wish we actually had gone to see Bob Holmes four years ago. Why didn't we?"

"Lots of reasons," Greg replied. "First, we were in such a state of shock after our parents were killed. It took me a while to get my head on straight. Then when I could function, I plunged into med school."

"Yeah, I was stunned, and just a kid barely out of college. I couldn't believe what happened to our folks. It was all so sudden and unreal, and, as you well know, I spent a couple of years wallowing in self-pity. Thinking about what was happening to the company was the furthest thing from my mind."

"Same with me," said Greg. "I just took it for granted that FerMon was doing all right—like it was always there and always would be."

"Yeah, we got our dividends and didn't give the company another thought. At least I didn't, not until I started the part-time job and got an earful."

"What are your thoughts about what we should do next?"

Sue took a bite of her salad, trying to buy a little time before she answered.

"Well, I think we both have to grow up pretty fast here," she finally said. "I'm 25. You're 26. And so far, we've been well taken care of financially. But now, things aren't looking all that good. We've got to pay attention to what's going on in this business. Not only that but we also have to give attention to it. And time. But we're in such a weird position."

"What do you mean?" Greg asked, but even as he asked, he knew what she would say.

"I mean this company is ours, but we don't control it until we're 30. I'm afraid it'll go down the tubes before we have a chance to take control. I know our parents meant well when they named Uncle Perry the trustee of our trusts. But he's a high school principal and, frankly, I don't think he knows much about running a business. He makes sure we get our dividends but when it comes to overseeing the voting stock, he seems to go along with whatever management wants. He's trustworthy and honest, and that's why our parents appointed him. But he doesn't seem to ask the right questions and he puts too much faith in management. Someone from the ownership side needs to be setting goals and making our family's expectations clear to management."

"That means us," said Greg.

"Yes, but without control over the voting stock, how do we do that?"

"We may not have outright control, but that doesn't mean we are without power," Greg said mysteriously.

It was Sue's turn to ask: "What do you mean?"

"It occurs to me that Bob Holmes gave us an extraordinary amount of ammunition this morning in the form of facts and information. We can begin to use it to bring about whatever change is necessary. As they say, knowledge is power."

"How would we proceed?" Sue asked. She was thinking about David Glenn, who had been named president of FerMon after their parents' deaths. "David and I don't get along all that well. I think he thinks of me as some snotty-nosed kid, the dreaded boss's daughter. I certainly wouldn't want to march into his office and demand answers to all the questions we've raised today."

"No, of course not," Greg agreed. "We need a more sophisticated approach, we need adequate preparation, and we need to build support. Do some coalition building, so to speak."

"What do you have in mind?"

"You and I both have a good relationship with Uncle Perry, right?" Greg didn't wait for an answer. "I think we start with him. For openers, I don't think he was all that comfortable with the idea of serving as trustee of the trusts, and I bet he was sure he'd never have to. Then the unthinkable happened and he was stuck with the job. He could have let the bank take over, as alternate trustee, but he would have felt too guilty. I think it's up to us to convince him that we're serious about wanting to be involved in the business and that we want to be responsible owners. We need to let him know what we've learned today and what our concerns are. I believe he'll welcome our interest and once we've got him in our corner, a whole lot of things can happen."

"Like what?"

"Well, for one thing, the three of us together will have that meeting with management—that is, with David Glenn—and we'll ask him to provide us with the answers to our questions and discuss our concerns," Greg said.

"What if we don't like what we hear?"

"I'll get to that, but let's not get too far ahead of ourselves. First things first. I also think we need to make it known to management that you and I will be attending board meetings, but for now only as observers. Neither of us has enough experience to be a board member, but observing meetings will certainly give us an education and help us understand what's going on."

"And speaking of the board," Sue interrupted, "my guess is that it's not the high-quality board we need. We've got David and one of the vice presidents and Uncle Perry. Then there's the company lawyer, the company's banker, and the company's CPA. And those three folks work for us already so they should already be giving us their knowledge and opinions. Why should they be on the board? I think we could use some top-drawer executives from some other companies—people who can help us turn FerMon around. With some nudging from us, Uncle Perry can make that happen."

"Great idea! How did you get so smart?"

Sue blushed. "I've been doing some reading."

"Obviously it's paying off," said Greg.

"Well, actually, I've got a surprise.

"A surprise?"

"I've enrolled in a family business leadership program at the university. It's a program that trains younger family members for leadership in their family businesses. I've also applied to several executive MBA programs and I think I have a good chance of being accepted."

"I can't believe this! My artsy cousin going for a business degree? Why? How?"

Sue smiled, pleased that she had so successfully astounded her cousin.

"Two things pushed me in this direction. You know as well as I do that when you grow up in a family business, business starts to seep into your blood," she said. "So, even when I was getting my art degree, I'd be thinking, 'How do I make this work as a business? How can I make a living at this?' The last thing my classmates were thinking about was how they would turn their passion into a viable business—so a lot of them have become starving artists who as work waiters and waitresses to support their art. Doctors, by the way, are also frequently terrible at business."

"Don't remind me," Greg said.

"The second reason is that working at FerMon, even on a part-time basis, really got my juices flowing," Sue went on. "I love this business. I began to see what a shame it would be if it didn't continue in the Monahan and Ferris families, and it took me a while to realize that I could be the link that keeps it going. An executive MBA program will allow me to continue to work in the company while I work on my degree on weekends. I know you want a medical career and I think that's wonderful. You shouldn't veer from that. But I also know that you love the company too. You'll be a great owner and, some day, a great board member."

Now Greg blushed. "Thanks."

"But I know I've got a lot of work ahead of me," Sue added. "A lot of work. Including getting people like David to take me seriously." She broke into laughter and, tugging at her long hair and gesturing at her flashy jewelry, she said, "I guess I'll have to get a new wardrobe and start looking the part. By the way, have you got some business suits? You will need them for board meetings."

"By the way yourself," Greg responded, grinning, "I was thinking about what Bob Holmes said about mentors. Do you have one?"

"No, but I'm looking for someone. Having one sure would help, but there's no one in the company right now that I can turn to. I think the university program can help me find someone outside the company who can guide me."

Sue paused a minute while she and Greg paid the bill.

"You still haven't said what we'll have to do if we don't like the answers we get from David Glenn," she said.

"I hate to say this, but we might need a new president," he said.

"I've been thinking the same thing. And that's what worries me. We've really got to have Uncle Perry on our side for that to happen."

"So we really have to do our homework with these financial statements and make sure he understands what we understand. We might even want to think about drawing in one of Uncle Perry's business friends to further convince him and to give us support."

"I have another suggestion," Sue said.

"Yes?"

"There are a lot of resources these days for family businesses, including consultants who work with family companies and help them with the sorts of things we're going through now. I think we ought to hire one."

"Sounds like a good idea."

"Also, in addition to the university program that I'm attending, there are seminars and groups for people like you and me who want to learn more about ownership and other aspects of family business. I'd really like it if we could start going to some of these meetings and learning more together. That way, we'll be on the same page."

"That sounds good to me, too," Greg said. "After all, as you said, this business does have to support me through medical school and help me set up my practice. After what it looks like we're going to have to go through, maybe I'll specialize in psychiatry."

Sue laughed and then grew quiet. "You know," she said, "I really hope we never have to sell this business."

"Me neither," said Greg. "I hope to have a family someday. I'd really love to pass this on to my kids."

Sue and Greg spent a few more minutes dividing initial tasks. They knew they had no time to waste. Sue would do some of the additional industry research Bob Holmes had suggested and Greg would review the financial statements and draft a presentation for Uncle Perry. He would also call

Perry and get a meeting set up for some time within the next 10 days. Sue also volunteered to gather the names of some family business consultants who might work well in the FerMon situation and she and Greg agreed to meet with each one until they settled on a choice. Greg also asked Sue to scout out some family business seminars that they could attend together and he agreed to read some books on family business that she had in her library.

As they walked out to the car after lunch, Greg put an arm around his cousin.

"You know what, Suze?" he said. "I really owe you one for initiating all this, even though I gave you a hard time at first. You were right to ask some questions about what's been going on. But more important, we're really lucky to be so close. Most cousins aren't so fortunate. I feel like you and I together can deal with whatever it is we have to face here."

Sue gave Greg a little hug. "Yep," she said.

Accounting Terms

Accounting period	The customary span of time for which an operating statement is prepared.
Accounting principles	The body of doctrine associated with the practice of accounting, serving as an explanation of current methods and as a guide in the selection of conventions and procedures.
Accounts payable	Total a business owes to its creditors.
Accounts receivable	A claim or amount due from a debtor.
Accrual	The recognition of income and expenses when they occur even if not received or paid for until later.
Accrual method	A method of accounting where all income earned and expenses incurred, prepaid or unpaid are assigned to specific periods of time.
Accumulated depreciation	The fixed-asset valuation account offsetting depreciation provisions.
Accrued expenses	Liability for expenses that have been incurred and are not paid but are payable at some future date.
Actual cost	Cost, as of acquisition or production, of the former net of discounts and allowances but including transportation and storage; often averaged for internal-transfer or inventory purposes.
Assets	Resources which have monetary value.
Bad debt	An account that cannot be collected.
Balance sheet	A statement of financial condition of a business at a certain date showing its assets, liabilities and capital.
Capital	The difference between a business owner's total assets and total liabilities; equity or investment.

Cash basis	Record keeping method whereby notation is made only of cash received or cash disbursed.
Cash flow	How the financial transactions for the period affect the company's cash.
Common stock	Stock, the ownership of which confers no special privileges; owners of such stock prevail after the company's liabilities and other proprietary claims have been satisfied.
Corporation	An entity created to do business in a state through its charter.
Cost basis	The valuation basis followed in recording and reporting expenditures
Cost of sales	The total cost of sales of goods sold during a given accounting period, determined by ascertaining for each item of sale the invoice and such other costs pertaining to the item as may have been included in the cost of goods purchased.
Credit	The ability to buy or borrow in consideration of a promise to pay within a period, sometimes loosely specified following delivery.
Creditor	One who is owned a debt of money or services.
Current asset	Assets that normally will be converted into cash within the year or sooner.
Current liabilities	The short-term debt of a business, normally payable within a year or sooner.
Depreciation	Wear and tear of a fixed asset which decreases its value.
Direct Cost	The cost of any good or service that contributes to and is readily ascribable to product or service output, any other cost incurred being regarded as a fixed or period cost.

Disclosure	An explanation, or exhibit, attached to a financial statement, or embodied in a report (e.g. an auditor's) containing a fact, opinion, or detail required or helpful in the interpretation of the statement or report; an expanded heading of a footnote.
Dividends	Profit distribution to shareholders.
Expenditure	The incurring of a liability, the payment of cash, or the transfer of property for the purpose of acquiring an asset or service or settling a loss.
FIFO	First in, first out, term used in costing of inventory; oldest acquisitions are disposed of first.
Financial statement	A presentation of financial data at a specific period in time.
First in, First Out	The inventory which is acquired earliest is assumed to be used first, the inventory acquired latest is assumed to be still on hand.
Fixed Asset	Assets with a useful life of more than one year.
GAAP	Generally accepted accounting principles.
Go public	Offer stock in the company to the public through a stock exchange.
Good will	The gross value of a business exceeding the book value.
Gross profit	Net sales less cost of goods sold.
Gross sales	Total sales, before deducting returns and allowances but after deducting corrections and trade discounts, sales taxes, excise taxes based on sales and sometimes cash discounts.
Income statement	A summary of the revenue and expenses for a specified period.
Intangible asset	Any "two-dimensional" or "incorporeal" asset; any asset other than cash or real estate; in this sense used by some tax authorities.

Inventory	Raw materials and supplies, goods finished and in process of manufacture and merchandise on hand, in transit and owned, in storage, or consigned to others at the end of an accounting period.
Liability	An amount owed by one person (debtor) to another person (or creditor).
Liquid Assets	Cash or items that you can readily convert to cash within a year.
Long-term debt	Term on balance sheet signifying debt due after one year.
Manufacturing expenses	All costs of manufacturing, not including raw materials and labor costs.
Margin	Gross profits.
Net sales	Gross sales minus returns and allowances.
Net worth	The total appearing on an accounting records of the equities representing proprietary interests. The going-concern value of assets over liabilities.
Operating expenses	The expenses a business incurs in its operation.
Overhead	Any cost of doing business other than a direct cost of an output of product or services.
Partnership	Arrangement whereby two or more people or entities merge forces so that each will benefit, with profits and losses shared jointly.
Prepaid expense	A type of deferred charge.
Profit and Loss Statement	The difference between income and expenses of a business for a period and the profit (or loss) resulting therefrom.
Raw materials	Component part of finished goods.
Receivables	Collectible, whether or not due.
Share	One of the units of equal value into which each class of the capital stock of a corporation is divided.
Shareholders' equity	Net worth. Also called owners' equity.

Sole Proprietorship	A business owned by one person.
Standard cost	A forecast or predetermination of what actual costs should be under projected conditions, serving as a basis of cost control and as a measure of productive efficiency.
Stock	Shares issued by a corporation, evidenced by formal certificates representing ownership in the corporation. The total amount of shares is know as the Capital Stock of the corporation.
Stockholder	The owner of shares of the capital stock of a corporation.
Terms	Conditions of payment.
Variable expenses	Expenses that vary closely with changes in sales volume.
Working capital	Capital currently used to operate the business. The excess of current assets over current liabilities.
Write off	To transfer the balance of an account previously regarded as an asset to an expense account or profit and loss.

INDEX

Accounting period 21, 99-100, 102
Accounts payable 17, 20, 26, 35-36, 57, 59-69, 77-79, 99
Accounts receivable..........6, 15, 17, 20-21, 26, 33, 36, 40, 45, 51, 55-56, 60-64, 68, 75, 78, 99
Accrual 17, 56, 65-66, 99
Accrued earnings 4
Accrued expenses..26, 45, 63-64, 99
Annual reports 1, 5-9, 13, 37, 71-72, 74, 85
Assets 19-24
Auditors 9-13

Balance sheet 13-36
Board of directors 3, 11
Book value 23, 27-28, 34, 89, 101
Break even 55, 82-84

C Corporation...45, 47
Capital...11, 14-15, 27-28, 35-36, 74-75, 99-103
Cash basis...17, 100
Cash cycle 76, 78-79
Cash flow statement 12, 36-38, 58-77
Cash shortage...33, 60, 62
Common stock 27-28, 100
Cost of sales 39, 41-42, 52, 55, 83, 100

Debentures 4
Debt-free...4
Debt to equity 79
Deferred taxes 27
Depreciation 22-23, 34, 36, 41-44, 65, 85, 99
Dividend payout ratio...80-81
Dividends 4, 12, 28, 38, 40, 45-46, 49-50, 59, 64, 66-69, 73, 80-81, 87, 89, 93-94, 101

EBITDA...85

FIFO 43, 101
Fixed assets 22-23, 25, 28, 33-36, 66-68, 72, 74, 85

GAAP 10, 101
General partnership 67
Good will 24, 28, 101

Income statement 9, 13, 22, 26, 32, 34, 36-38, 49, 51, 59-69, 76, 80, 83, 85, 101
Insurance premiums 21, 56
Intangible assets...24, 34
Interest coverage ratio 80
Inventory 9-10, 15, 20-21, 23, 33, 36-37, 42-43, 51-53, 61-62,
                          68, 72, 74, 76-78, 83, 88, 91-92, 99, 101-102
Inventory turns...76, 88

105

Leveraging 16, 35, 65, 99
Liabilities...25-29, 35-36
Limited liability company 47
Limited liability partnership...47
Limited partnership 47
Liquidity 35-36, 60, 64, 71-73, 79

Margins 53, 57, 82, 85-87, 92
Mentor 3, 96

Net sales 6-8, 39-40, 51-53, 55, 69, 75, 83-87, 101
Net working capital 74-75, 79
Notes payable 25, 61, 66

Operating expenses........................7, 39, 41, 44-45, 53-55, 57, 82-83, 86, 91-92, 102
Operating income 57, 85-86
Owners' equity...15, 37, 102
    see also shareholders' equity

Payable turns..77-78
Prepaid expenses 21-22, 33-34, 63-64, 73
Profit and loss...37, 102-103

Receivable turns..75, 91
Retained earnings 11, 28-29, 35, 37-38, 45, 64, 89
Return on assets..88
Return on equity 89
Returns and allowances...40, 53, 76, 91, 101-102

S Corporation...45, 47, 66, 69, 80
Sales growth 81-82
Shareholders' equity 14-15, 28, 102
    see also Owners' equity
Short-term loans 26, 33, 35, 60, 62
Sole proprietorship 47, 103

Times interest earned ratio 80

Variable expenses 55, 103

Working capital..36, 74-75, 103
Write off 21, 56, 103